START TALKING TO YOUR KIDS ABOUT SEX

"Christian parents are asking for resources to help them better parent their children, especially in the areas of sexuality and gender. Julia Sadusky provides parents with so much of what they seek. This book is a rich resource grounded in Christian doctrine and wisdom while simultaneously being accessible and practical. The range of scenarios Sadusky covers and the practical insights and suggestions she offers will be invaluable to parents."

Mark A. Yarhouse
Dr. Arthur P. Rech and Mrs. Jean May Rech Professor of Psychology
Wheaton College

"For parents who are worried about the inherent risks of raising children in our time, this book offers solid tools that can help prevent abuse and appropriately remove a naivety that can no longer be accepted. Trustworthy, honest, and unpretentious, this is the right book at the right time. Convicting and empowering! A must-read for parents and the perfect gift for newlyweds."

Very Rev. R. Michael Dollins
Vicar general of the Archdiocese of Denver

"An invaluable resource for anyone who desires proactive and practical ways to talk about sexuality with young children. Julia Sadusky combines her years of experience and current research to guide and support important parenting conversations about sexuality, safety, and health during early developmental milestones. Her faith and strengths shine through with encouraging and vital information for children's holistic health and wellness."

Deborah Watson
Clinical Assistant Professor
Institute of Pastoral Studies

"Julia Sadusky brings her experience as a licensed psychologist to help parents be proactive in leading conversations with their children about the beauty of God's gift of our sexuality. Filled with practical advice, we've been blessed as parents by Sadusky's timely and important work!"

Jackie and Bobby Angel
Catholic authors and speakers

"This book is a solidly Catholic treasure trove of practical wisdom. I'm already thinking about how to apply these tips and strategies with my own kids. Sadusky has given us a much-needed map to navigate the trickiest of topics with clarity, confidence, and gentleness."

Abigail Favale
Professor in the McGrath Institute for Church Life
University of Notre Dame

"Many parents struggle with how to talk with their children about their bodies and sexuality, especially with society promoting so many worldviews that reject the natural law. Julia Sadusky's eminently practical book tackles this tough topic in an accessible and faithfully Catholic way. You won't regret taking even a few moments to learn from her insight and experience."

Archbishop Samuel J. Aquila
Archdiocese of Denver

"This book is what I have been searching for as a school counselor and a mother! It is a concise and direct roadmap to follow as you have crucial conversations with children about sex, their bodies, boundaries, and more. Sadusky provides processing tools to work through as you anticipate how to respond to children's natural curiosity around sex without shame. An absolute must-read for parents, teachers, school counselors, and all those who work with children!"

Jasmyn Joubert
Counselor at Crowley High School
Lafayette, Louisiana

START TALKING TO YOUR KIDS ABOUT SEX

A PRACTICAL GUIDE FOR CATHOLICS

JULIA SADUSKY

Ave Maria Press AVE Notre Dame, Indiana

Nihil Obstat: David Uebbing, MA
Censor Librorum

Imprimatur: Most Reverend Samuel J. Aquila, STL
Archbishop of Denver
Given at Denver, Colorado, on May 5, 2023

Founded in 1865, Ave Maria Press is a ministry of the United States Province of Holy Cross.

www.avemariapress.com

Paperback: ISBN-13 978-1-64680-222-7

E-book: ISBN-13 978-1-64680-223-4

Cover image © gettyimages.com.

Cover and text design by Brian C. Conley.

Printed and bound in the United States of America.

Library of Congress Cataloging-in-Publication Data

Names: Sadusky, Julia, author.
Title: Start talking to your kids about sex : a practical guide for Catholics / Julia Sadusky.
Description: Notre Dame, Indiana : Ave Maria Press, [2023] | Includes bibliographical references and index. | Summary: "A Catholic-Christian, non-shaming, holistic guide to talking to kids about sex and sexuality"-- Provided by publisher.
Identifiers: LCCN 2023020650 (print) | LCCN 2023020651 (ebook) | ISBN 9781646802227 (paperback) | ISBN 9781646802234 (ebook)
Subjects: LCSH: Sex instruction for children--Religious aspects--Catholic Church. | Child rearing--Religious aspects--Catholic Church.
Classification: LCC HQ53 .S227 2023 (print) | LCC HQ53 (ebook) | DDC 372.37/2--dc23/eng/20230712
LC record available at https://lccn.loc.gov/2023020650
LC ebook record available at https://lccn.loc.gov/2023020651

TO MY GODCHILDREN:
NOAH, MAGGIE, LILABET, JOSEPHINE, AND LILLIAN.
MAY YOUR LIGHT SHINE WHEREVER YOU GO, AND
MAY YOU BE KEPT SAFE FROM EVERY EVIL.

THE BEST INHERITANCE A PARENT CAN GIVE HIS CHILDREN IS A FEW MINUTES OF HIS TIME EACH DAY.

—O. A. BATTISTA

CONTENTS

ACKNOWLEDGMENTS

This book came out of countless conversations with dear friends, family, and clients who are willing to be honest about and courageously face the day-to-day challenges of parenting. Thank you, in a particular way, to Sarah Silva and Catie and Will Panagakos, for trusting me with questions about how to protect your kids from harm and love them well, even when it means talking about things that make us want to scream! Your reflections and questions gave birth to this book project. Thank you also to Meghan Suchomski, Maggie Maslak, and Dr. Dara Houp, for your friendship, for your endless encouragement, and for being a haven for musings about raising healthy and sexually whole children. I am deeply grateful for your witnesses of motherhood. You, along with your husbands, Chris Suchomski, Eric Maslak, and Will Houp, are the kind of parents this world needs more of.

Thank you to Danielle Syrup and Erin Worth, for putting up with my almost daily musings about all the ways we can do better as Christians and for living with me in this precious season of life. And thank you to the many reviewers who took the time to give feedback along the way: Dr. Steven Gros, Lauren Accolla, Dr. Mark Yarhouse, Chris Damian, Anna Heling, and Johnny Sapienza.

Thank you to my siblings and in-laws, Robert and Katherine Sadusky, Lauren Tibbets, Zachary and Stephanie Sadusky, Maria Sadusky, Oliver and Therese Lawrence, Luke Sadusky, and Matthew Sadusky. With each passing day, I become more aware of the absolute gift you are to me. To be surrounded by so many brave, strong, and faithful souls in one family is something few people can claim. I would not want to face the peaks and valleys without you. Finally, thank you to my parents, Bob and Lynne, for raising me and giving me six siblings to learn from and grow with. Mom, you were right, we really did all become best friends.

Working with Ave Maria Press has been a dream. Kristi McDonald offered infectious excitement for this project and gave invaluable feedback at every turn. Dr. Gregory Coles was there in the early stages, believing in my ability to write this book when it was still a pipe dream, and offered edits that only he could.

A book like this would never have happened without the trust and vulnerability of so many loved ones and clients, especially those who have survived egregious traumas. To each one of you, I will never tire of saying it: You are good. It was not your fault. You have taught me more than you realize, and you deserve the very best this life can offer and even more in the life to come. You inspire me and call me on to be a better human, to stand up against injustice, to speak out when I see the warning signs of abuse, and to do what little I can to make the world safer for generations to come. Don't believe the rumors. Your light is a force this world needs. Stay.

INTRODUCTION

WHY "THE TALK" WAS NEVER ENOUGH

On the other end of the phone, Janelle was frantic and upset. When she had walked into her family's playroom earlier that afternoon, she found her five-year-old son, Benjamin, touching his own penis while pointing to his three-year-old brother's penis. Both boys were laughing.

"I didn't know what to say or do," Janelle told me. "I froze. I don't think I handled it right, but I grabbed Benjamin's hand and swatted it away from touching himself. I told them, 'Stop that right now. It's not funny.' I know I embarrassed them, because their faces were beet-red. Benjamin won't even look me in the eye. What do I do now?"

If we're honest, we have all been Janelle in one moment or another. We can all look back on a way we've handled an interaction and recognize that we panicked and overreacted. For Janelle, seeing Benjamin touching his penis led her to react out of fear. For others, it might be trying to respond to a question from a child about where babies come from. For others, this same kind of fear reaction might be sparked when our kid asks us a question about sexual intercourse or about a same-sex couple they know.

All of us need help in raising children who are holy, healthy, and faithful. I've seen this time and time again as a therapist working with Christian families. The following questions arise:

- Where can we turn to figure out responses to questions like these?
- What guidance can we trust?
- How early is too early to talk about genitalia, the body, and sex?
- When is it too late?
- And ultimately, how do we be proactive instead of reactive when it comes to guiding our children toward a healthy sense of themselves as whole and integrated humans, made in the image of God?

Not sure? You're not alone.

In my research, I found that there are very few, if any, resources that help parents answer these questions. One of the websites that *does* offer specific suggestions for talking to kids about sexuality is the Planned Parenthood website. While they have some helpful information, many aspects of their approach won't resonate with Christian parents.

All that is to say, this book is long overdue. For too long, our broader Western culture has believed that Christians are afraid or ashamed of the human body, rejecting it, unable to acknowledge ourselves as sexual beings. And these critiques aren't completely unwarranted. So many people I've spoken to about their upbringing in Christian homes have told me that sexuality was never talked about. If their parents did talk about it, they focused on "what not to do," and even these conversations only tended to happen once. There was little room for kids to learn about their bodies, which kinds of exploratory play and touch are normal and which are out of bounds, and what to do when someone else violates their body's boundaries. The lack of these conversations often led to all kinds of difficulties down the road.

My passion to write this book is informed by my own years of research and teaching about sexual development and gender and sexual identity formation. As a licensed psychologist who is also a committed Christian—and as a Catholic woman in particular—I see so much opportunity for Catholics and other Christians to better engage these conversations about sexuality and gender. Our failure to engage well in these conversations has significant consequences on so many lives, even more than we realize.

I have sat for hours with clients recalling experiences of childhood sexual abuse or sexual experiences that led to confusion and enormous shame. Most of my clients felt they couldn't possibly have gone to their parents or other caregivers to discuss their experiences and feelings. Many shared that, even as children, they sensed their parents' fear, shame, embarrassment, and conflicted feelings about their own sexual desires and experiences. My clients didn't bring up their questions or experiences out of a desire to protect their parents. As a result, tragically, these parents were never given the opportunity to protect their children.

A lack of conversation about sexuality in the home is a common precursor to sexual addiction, early sexual activity, and sexual abuse.[1] I want to help parents and educators be proactive in addressing sexuality to better protect children and equip them for healthy and whole lives. It is heart-wrenching to hear again and again how well-meaning adults avoided talking about sexuality, not wanting to "scandalize" a child. That child then believed they ought to keep unwanted experiences or confusing thoughts and feelings to themselves, or turned to pornography, peers, sexual partners, or abusive adults to educate them.

I hope this book will help you build confidence to discuss sexuality in developmentally appropriate ways. I hope it will help you move past your fears and insecurities in talking to your kids. In doing so, you can help your children feel freedom to talk about their bodies and their sexuality with you. Perhaps we can raise a generation who will bring their questions to parents, their primary educators, and other trusted adults with boldness and ease.

You may be wondering by now, "Who is this book for?" The primary audience is parents who are seeking to raise children who are healthy and holy adults one day. While a lot of the examples I give in this book will incorporate families where both parents are in the home, I know some readers will be single parents as well, and I want to acknowledge the specific sacrifices and steadfastness you demonstrate daily as you tackle parenting.

Beyond parents, this book is for anyone seeking to understand how to better engage with children (and yourself) around sexuality. This includes Christians who are teachers, children's ministry staff, godparents, nannies, priests, and religious brothers and sisters. Not every example will cleanly apply to every situation, but my hope is that this book gives you some direction and can spur the development of other resources in the future.

If you're a parent or another caregiver taking the time to sit down and read this book, thank you! (As if you don't have enough to do!) If you can muster the time to read the whole book from cover to cover, that will equip you with the most thorough vision for parenting your child or assisting children in your care. But I recognize that many of you might be juggling so many responsibilities that you feel as if you barely have the chance to take a breath, let alone read a book. If you can't get to the whole book, focus on the chapters that are most relevant to your child.

This book, which is book 1 in a two-book series, is structured around ten of the most significant questions I receive from parents and educators who want to know how to talk with children aged zero to nine about sexuality. Book 2 will focus on ten other significant questions that apply to raising children aged ten to eighteen. It will discuss puberty, sexual attraction, and behaviors, building on the foundation book 1 provides. The format of both books is meant to make it easily accessible for you as parents and educators who, at different phases of child development, face different questions regarding talking about sexuality. The earlier chapters offer general guidelines for working with children in various developmental stages, while the later chapters deal more with specific situations and concerns related to navigating sleepovers, coaching kids to respond to unwanted touch, and so on.

If you have a child aged zero to two, I'd begin with chapters 1 and 2. Chapter 1 helps with identifying barriers to starting conversations with children about their bodies, and chapter 2 explains why we use medical terms for genitalia when talking to children, rather than nicknames. Chapter 3 will apply to children aged three to six, since it will address the natural growing curiosity about the body at that time. If you have a child who is starting at school, daycare, or another venue outside the home, you may want to prioritize chapters 3 to 5, which help you teach a child how to engage with adults and children outside the home. Even if you only have five minutes a day to spend with this book, look for one piece of practical advice you can apply to help you strengthen your relationship with your child and their relationship with their body.

Be patient with yourself as you move through these pages. Some of the content will be difficult and will invite you to self-reflect in meaningful but painful ways. This process will be worthwhile, but pace yourself as you need to. As we begin, remember that "It is the LORD who goes before you; he will be with you, he will not fail you or forsake you; do not fear or be dismayed" (Deuteronomy 31:8).

You do not need to be a therapist or a trained professional to help your children grow a healthy relationship with their bodies. At the end of the day, you are more capable than you realize, and I hope that you will become increasingly confident in your abilities with each passing day.

CHAPTER 1

"WHY AM I HAVING SUCH A HARD TIME STARTING THE CONVERSATION?"

OVERCOMING BARRIERS TO DISCUSSING SEXUALITY

A question I ask nearly every adult client I meet with at some point in our work is this: "When did you first learn about your body?" Most of them will recall memories after a few moments. They may mention a time when they noticed their body as different from the body of an opposite-sex sibling or friend, a time when they touched their anatomy to see what it was all about, or a time when they experienced unwanted sexual touch.

Then I ask a question that is often much harder to answer: "Who taught you about your body?" Many of my clients will say that no one did. Others say they learned about their body from pornography, from a peer, or from a person who sexually violated them.

The third question I ask really stumps most people: "What lessons did your parents teach you about your body and sexuality?" Nearly all my clients, many of whom are Christians, look puzzled when I ask. Some literally say, "Nothing." Others might say, "My parents didn't talk about sex." Or, "I walked in on them having sex one time and put two and two together, but we never talked about those things. It would've been too awkward for everyone."

Others recall receiving "the talk" right around puberty. Maybe a parent showed them a diagram of anatomy, offered them birth control or condoms, or simply blushed and said, "Sex is natural. You'll figure it out when you get married."

Without the guidance of parents or other trustworthy adults, my clients typically "figured it out" on their own, which means that by the time they were adults, the internet, magazines, health class, friends, or a crush had given them their education. And this created more problems than it solved.

Waiting until puberty to talk about sexuality is too late. Kids, even infants, are already on a journey of sexual development, even though sexuality is not front and center in their minds. Children touch their genitalia as a common part of their childhood development, and their early experiences and understandings of their own bodies are critical for healthy sexual development into adulthood. But even when adults understand these things, we still tend to wait as long as possible to initiate conversations about sexuality with children. Why do we wait?

WHAT GETS IN THE WAY?

Before we dive into the how-to of talking to your kids about sexuality, it's worth naming some of the common barriers that keep people from stepping into these conversations with their children early and often. Only once we've identified the barriers holding us back can we pray for the courage and seek the education to overcome these barriers.

Though many of the barriers parents face are distinct to their own experiences, one barrier is shared by the vast majority of parents who are reluctant to have this conversation. Put simply, a parent's own sexual education will impact their comfort and readiness to talk about sexuality with their children. Wanting to talk about sexuality, and even seeing the importance in doing so, can only take a person so far.

Think back to when you first began thinking about and then talking about sex. Who did you talk to? Who first taught you things about your anatomy, sexual intercourse, pleasure, boundaries? Did anyone teach you these things? Or did you have to teach yourself?

Some of you may have robust stories of ongoing conversations in your family about the body, sexuality, and the beautiful ways God uses our bodies to glorify him. My guess, though, is that most of you look back on childhood and cannot think of many chances to talk about sex in an open and non-shaming way.

This lack of adequate education can send all kinds of false messages about sexuality. Here are some of the common false messages that many of us have carried into adulthood.

- Sexuality is all bad outside of marriage, and all good in it. My parents said that, and that was all that needed to be said. Just teach kids what not to do and the rest will come later.
- Sexuality is dirty or shameful, and it ought to be treated with suspicion because it can lead to sin.
- Sexuality will be taught to my kids through my church or school system. I trust them to do that better than I could.
- Sexuality is inappropriate to talk about with other people.
- Sexuality is something to hide away and keep to myself. Other people don't wnt to hear about it, especially if I am doing something "wrong."
- Sexuality isn't something my parents wanted to talk about, and I needed to protect them (and everyone else) from that conversation because I didn't want to make them uncomfortable.
- Sexuality is so mysterious and sacred that, if human beings follow well-known moral commands, our sexual relationships and an adequate understanding of our bodies will come naturally. We don't *need* to talk about it.

When the time comes to talk about sexuality and to bring it into the open, in a marriage or with our own children, we are trying to exercise a muscle we have never used. This is our dilemma.

At some point, we all need to talk about sexuality. When we don't know how, many of us end up feeling guilty. We don't ask questions, because we think we ought to know the answers by now. Sometimes we feel resentful of our upbringing and reject the moral teachings we were raised within, blaming them for the poor education we received. We might try to avoid the conversation as long as we can, hoping that someday in the future we will be ready for it. This avoidance keeps us stuck in place, causing us to repeat the same cycle of silence we inherited from our own parents or caregivers.

One of my clients put it this way:

> "I was shocked that I felt embarrassment when I thought about bringing up anatomy to my little girl. I always thought of myself as 'healthy' in how I approached sex. She asked me one time what 'that thing' is between her baby brother's legs, and I blushed. I laughed because I was nervous and said, 'I will tell you when you are older.' I thought I wouldn't have to talk about all that until she was a teenager. But honestly, I just had no clue what to say back. So, I said nothing."

OTHER COMMON REASONS FOR SILENCE

These are some of the most common reasons parents tell me for why they don't talk to their kids about sexuality, or only do so around puberty.

- "I am afraid of doing harm to my children by talking about sex and the body too soon. I was exposed to sexual content in conversations with older siblings and friends prematurely, and that was uncomfortable to me. So, I stay silent because I don't want to overwhelm my child like I felt overwhelmed."
- "I don't have any helpful resources or good role models out there, so I stay silent because I don't want to say the wrong thing. I know I want to say something, but I am not sure what exactly to say, when to say it, and how. And I don't have enough hours in the day to track down information I can trust. Then life goes on, time passes, and nothing gets said."
- "I feel shame and embarrassment about my body and my own impulses. To talk in a neutral way about the body and sexuality with my child would make me confront my own gut reaction to the body, where I think I would feel things like disgust and anxiety. I hope it will get better as they get older."

- "I don't think it is on my kid's mind. They never say anything about their body and so I don't want to bring it up until they do."
- "I have some books I got from a friend that talk about how to talk about sex and puberty with teens. I don't see similar books for other age ranges, so I am guessing it's not necessary to talk sooner."
- "I was shamed in my childhood for my own exploration of my body. A parent came in when I was touching my genitals and they yelled at me. When my child does something similar, I don't want to say anything because I am afraid that I will have the same impact others had on me, and I don't want to be punitive or embarrass my child."
- "I was sexually abused as a kid. When the topic of sex comes up, I don't know what to say. I freeze up. I try not to talk about my child's body. Ignoring it may not be the best thing, but I get so stuck even thinking about talking about it. I get mad when my child runs naked into a room with guests in our house. I am so afraid about what could happen to them. I just do not know what to say or do."
- "I have struggled with and am still struggling with porn. It's something I got into when I was a teenager, and it's a habit that has been hard to break. I feel like an imposter. My kids will need to learn from someone else; who am I to try to help them?"

There are many barriers to stepping into these conversations, no doubt. And they all make sense, when we think about them in the context of our individual stories. Do any of these barriers resonate for you? Perhaps several do. Consider the following as a bit of "homework":

- If you can, take some time to share these barriers with someone you trust, maybe your spouse or a therapist or a close friend.
- As you reflect on these barriers, work to extend yourself grace and compassion in the challenges you have faced.
- Then see if you can imagine what it would look like and feel like to overcome these barriers. Imagine being confident as you initiate conversations with a child and feeling proud of the role you get to take in their life. Imagine being what you needed from

a parent or caregiver years ago. Before too long, my hope is that this image will become a reality.

If we don't broach these conversations early and often, what will happen to our kids? It seems that our world (and in some cases the worst members of it) will educate our children for us, with or without our consent or awareness. If we do not take concrete steps to learn, step outside of our comfort zones, and begin to take responsibility for their well-being in this concrete way, we will continue to face significant challenges as families and faith communities in passing on an understanding of sexuality that is life-giving and sustainable.

A CATHOLIC VISION FOR HUMAN SEXUALITY

As Christians, we have a beautiful and rich theology that highlights the value of our bodies. Catholics in particular have emphasized the importance of discovering the "theology" of our bodies—the ways our bodies communicate truths about who God is and who we are as people.[1] We profess that the human body is good and beautiful, and each embodied person is made in the image and likeness of the invisible God. We even believe that each and every human person reveals something to us about God and his love for his people. We reflect on the bodies of saints as sacred and worth venerating, to the point that we often seem odd to others when we travel to see relics. We believe that the human body, in its maleness and femaleness, is a sign of our ultimate purpose: communion with God and others! In and through our sexed bodies, we are able to give and receive love and create new life in some cases.[2] In and through our bodies, we are invited to be "a dwelling for the Most Holy Trinity."[3]

We joyfully declare that Jesus, the Son of God, took on flesh, becoming a man and thus elevating humanity and allowing us to reflect further on the dignity of our personhood, and that he came to redeem us in and through a human body in his Passion, Death, and Resurrection.[4] "It is in Christ, Redeemer and Savior, that the divine image, disfigured in man by the first sin, has been restored to its original beauty and ennobled by the grace of God."[5]

In our lives, though, we end up confronting the shame that we carry because of the Fall. We, like Adam and Eve in the garden, are naked and ashamed, in our own times and in our own ways.[6] This original shame paralyzes us and leads us to hide, not just from one another, but perhaps also from our children. Maybe one reason many adults wait as long as possible to discuss sexuality with children is that it triggers our own feelings of shame. We cover ourselves in fig leaves, even the fig leaves of solid theological frameworks and moral teachings, in the hopes that no one will notice our shame. The problem is this:

Our children can tell.

WHO TAUGHT YOU?

Let me ask you again, who first taught you about your body? How did you learn what it means to be a sexual being made in the image and likeness of God? Once you answer that question, we can consider what it looks like to talk to your own children about their bodies in a way that honors them as embodied souls, as beautiful reflections of God.

If your experience is anything like the experience of most Christians, you learned about the body in one of a few ways. Some of you remember a "talk" with one or both parents when your body was starting to change and develop around puberty. Some of you remember a friend or sibling or parent teaching you what pads and tampons are for and how they work. Others remember jokes in the locker room or at sleepovers about erections, wet dreams, and porn. Some of you don't remember even one conversation with parents about your body. You only remember that one time when you touched something on your body or someone else's body as a kid because you were curious; maybe your hand got slapped and you were told "No!" by an adult, with no further explanation. Still others received an "education" about sex and the body from pornographic images or videos, from *Playboy* magazines, or by receiving naked images from a crush. Some of you, tragically, were taught about your bodies in encounters with people who violated you, abused you, and took advantage of you for selfish gain. For that, I am deeply sorry. What happened to you was not okay.

If you want to make the most of this opportunity, here's my challenge to you: instead of seeking out one extensive conversation with your child, have many small conversations in the course of your daily life. As one friend of mine has said, "Have one hundred one-minute conversations, instead of one one-hundred-minute conversation." If you only have one talk (or no talks!) with your child about sex and their bodies, you simply won't have enough time to do any of it justice! In fact, if you wait until a child is hitting puberty, you may miss out on many valuable opportunities to teach your kids essential lessons that equip them for healthy and whole lives.

UNDERSTANDING CHILD SEXUAL DEVELOPMENT

A word on child sexual development will help us here. Humans are sexual beings. Children, then, are developing into sexual beings. By this I mean, children have bodies with sexual organs. Sure, they don't often think about their bodies as overtly sexual. And certainly, we want to protect them from premature exposure to sexual content (more on that later). But they are still developing sexual beings.

It is well understood that children are also curious about their bodies, specifically as they move through different developmental stages. Around ages three to five, most children begin to notice distinctions between boys' and girls' bodies. They sometimes want to play doctor, and if you are like most of the parents I know, engaging with kids around this type of exploration can be tough to navigate. Children express curiosity about childbirth and pregnancy and will often ask questions long before their own bodies move through puberty. This isn't because they are obsessed with sex. It's because they are genuinely curious!

Just like we gradually equip children to learn language, etiquette, and cultural expectations about many facets of life, we can equip them through practice to learn the language of their body and sexuality in developmentally appropriate ways. We don't wait for a child to ask us to teach them about nose-picking, chewing with their mouth open, or math. If we did, they would likely never learn those things.

PREVENTING ABUSE

Many parents ask me if they absolutely need to talk with their kids about sexuality before puberty. This is where we need to consider current research on child sexual abuse. I recognize that it's painful to acknowledge and face the reality of this evil. You may have your own story of experiencing sexual abuse as a child—if not, you almost certainly know someone who has been hurt in this way. Please take your time as you move through this, and be gentle with yourself as best you can.

Child sexual abuse is far too common. By age eighteen, one in ten children has experienced sexual abuse, with one in seven girls and one in twenty-five boys experiencing this.[7] Twenty percent of sexually abused children are abused prior to age eight, with the most children being abused between the ages of seven and thirteen.[8] This means that teaching children about their bodies, what those bodies are for, and who is allowed to have access to them can't wait until puberty. By age eight, one in every five abused children has already been hurt, and many have likely carried this emotional pain alone. Initiating conversations about sexuality signals that you are equipped to receive a child's story of abuse, excruciating as it may be to hear.

In some cases, having age-appropriate conversations about sexuality and body boundaries can also help prevent abuse. Only 10 percent of children abused are abused by a stranger.[9] About 40 percent of those sexually abused are abused by an older child.[10] This means that if we assume kids only need to set boundaries with strangers (by relying on rules like "don't talk to strangers"), we are making a huge mistake. Preventing abuse as effectively as possible means having countless conversations about boundaries, especially as children spend more time with adults and other children without their parents present.

If you knew that it was worth it to step into this challenging conversation, would you try to overcome the barriers you have been facing? If it meant better protecting children from abuse, teaching them sexual values that will sustain them in relationships for years to come, and modeling behavior they can use if they become parents one day, would it be worth giving this a shot?

TAKING STEPS FORWARD

1. Acknowledge that we have limitations.
2. Be curious about the barriers that hold us back.
3. Identify the thoughts and feelings that are getting in the way.
4. Proactively educate and cope.

As we begin to face our own limitations, we can find a path forward by taking a few simple steps. First, we want to **acknowledge** that we have limitations. Denial does us no favors when it comes to working on our difficulties. Second, we want to **be curious** about what might be getting in the way. By adopting a posture of curiosity—and with the support of a therapist, trusted friends, or a spouse—we can then **identify** the thoughts and feelings that are getting in our way. These might include any of the thoughts we described earlier, often accompanied by feelings of shame, guilt, disgust, inadequacy, inefficacy, anxiety, or paralysis. Once we have identified the thoughts and feelings that are making it difficult to step into conversations about sexuality, we can begin to **proactively educate** ourselves and learn to **cope with** the difficult thoughts and feelings we are facing, without hiding away in whatever fig leaves we've grabbed along the way.

If you're reading this book, you're already on the path toward proactive education—that's what the next nine chapters are for! When it comes to coping, the kinds of strategies that help you most will depend on what typical thoughts and feelings you are getting "stuck" in. Of course, nothing I say here is a substitute for therapy. As a person who goes to therapy myself, I can't say enough about how helpful high-quality therapy can be. But given that there are often barriers to accessing therapy, I want to give you a few starting points for coping with the challenges you might experience as you approach these topics with your children.

Before I do so, it's worth saying more about why coping skills are so important. Coping skills help humans when we find ourselves in moments when we feel at our wit's end. The way you might think about this is that each of us has a "window of tolerance." If something happens in our day that stresses us out or upsets us, it can make our window of tolerance smaller. If something positive happens, like a job promotion or other good news, it can expand our window of tolerance (so that things like traffic or a slow line at the grocery store don't get under our skin as much).

The good news is, we don't have to totally depend on environmental circumstances to determine our window of tolerance. There are actually skills we can learn that widen our window of tolerance. This means that on hard days or in preparing for difficult conversations, we can use these skills to help us handle what may otherwise feel impossible. So, for all the conversations you are preparing for through this book, remember the following skills are concrete strategies you can learn more about now. Trust me, they will make things easier on you, and you deserve that. Isn't life is hard enough already?

- *Relaxation techniques* are incredibly valuable when you are feeling anxious and overwhelmed. These include things like deep breathing, prayer, times of silence in Eucharistic Adoration, and the practice of lectio divina. Make sure that you have stressful or longer conversations only after you have done something that relaxes you, such as taking a bath, going for a walk, listening to songs from a favorite playlist, sitting outside in the sunshine, enjoying a favorite beverage, or taking even a few moments to breathe.
- *Emotional regulation skills*—that is, anything you do that brings down the intensity of your feelings even slightly—can be helpful. Mindfulness is a common effective skillset that can take on many forms. This involves remaining connected to the present moment, noticing the thoughts and feelings that "wash" over you, and focusing on noticing these thoughts and feelings without trying to "do anything" about them. Doing this exercise in self-awareness while breathing deeply allows you to shift your attention back and forth between your thoughts and feelings and your breath. This is especially important—and especially difficult—when your thoughts are really "loud" and your feelings are so intense that it's difficult to think clearly. With practice, you can grow in your ability to stay aware of your thoughts and feelings without being overwhelmed by them.
- *Try reframing* the conversations with your kids about their bodies and sexuality as opportunities to grow, rather than moments you dread. It is worth mentioning that, when you face the things that cause you anxiety, the anxiety will gradually recede. So, facing hard conversations willingly, early, and often will be so worth it in the long run. Remember, too, that when you step into these

spaces with your children, you are being what every child needs. What is more important than that?

- *Positive self-talk* allows you to tweak the way you talk to yourself in difficult moments or conversations with your kids. Notice the common ways you engage with yourself around your difficult thoughts and feelings. What kind of messages are you telling yourself, either explicitly or implicitly? Is that how you would talk to a friend if you wanted to encourage them to take a risk? Is that how you would motivate a child to do what you want them to do? Work on telling yourself the truth rather than being overly optimistic: "This is difficult, *and* you will make it through. Your feelings are valid, *and* they will not always be this strong. This is scary or uncomfortable, *and* it is an opportunity to grow."
- *Environment management strategies* are ways of setting up yourself and your environment for better and more productive conversations. This could mean only having conversations with your kids about sexuality in a quiet place that feels calm—a place where you won't be interrupted—or scheduling time when you know you won't be as tired or overwhelmed as you might be otherwise. It could also mean doing an activity with your child that you enjoy or going for a drive together rather than making "talking" the sole focus of the time.

In the chapters that follow, you will be proactively educating yourself so you can show up for your children with confidence, ease, and clarity. Let's turn now to talking about bodies and how we can explain them to children with ease.

CHAPTER 2

"WHAT IS THIS?"

IDENTIFYING AND EXPLAINING GENITALIA

How do we talk about body parts—specifically, genitalia—with children? As you move through this chapter, you will learn the importance of using anatomical terms for body parts instead of nicknames. I will offer some recommendations for explaining the purpose of different body parts to a young child. You will also gain insight into the best times to begin these conversations with children. And just as importantly, you will learn ways to figure out when initiating conversations will be helpful for your kid and when it's likely to overwhelm them with information that will be too much for them.

HOW TO TALK ABOUT GENITALIA

There are all kinds of nicknames people tend to use when talking about a child's anatomy, specifically their genitals. You have likely heard some of them: wee-wee, pee-pee, bum, heinie, and so on. Words like these are often encouraged as more "polite" or "appropriate" to use in public. In fact, a friend of mine recently shared with me that her kids, who use terms like "penis" and "vagina," have been corrected multiple times by their daycare and told to say "wee-wee" and "pee-pee" instead. Sometimes, when parents talk about the body to children, they may even notice themselves whispering, as if what they're saying is something secret or taboo. We must ask ourselves: "What message does this send a child?"

Using accurate medical terms with children communicates valuable information. It tells them that these body parts are good and normal to talk about with trusted people. It can allow for a neutral dialogue about the function of different body parts at different stages of a child's life, and, most importantly, it can help to prevent sexual abuse.

Read that again. Using accurate medical terms for anatomy can help to prevent abuse. How does this work? Stay tuned, and we'll discuss it later in this chapter.

For now, I want to point out that children who are not taught accurate language for their genitals can get the message that certain parts of their body shouldn't be talked about because they are something to be ashamed of. When we choose to adjust our language to nicknames, it is worth asking, "Who am I using this language for?" Is it for me as a parent, because I feel uncomfortable with identifying anatomy, including my own? Is it out of fear of things being overheard in public, and what other parents would think if they heard my son name his penis out loud?

Imagine this scenario happening to you: you're in a public place, and your child loudly uses an anatomical name for their genitals. Notice what feelings come up for you when you imagine this. Do you feel anxious, embarrassed, or uncertain? Comfortable and at ease?

Now read the following words out loud. (Unless you are sitting in public, that is—not everyone has learned as much as you have about the importance of being comfortable with this conversation!)

- Penis
- Vagina
- Scrotum
- Testicles
- Sperm
- Vulva
- Hymen
- Clitoris

Take note of what it feels like to read those terms out loud. This will help you gauge your own comfort level when it comes to teaching your children about their bodies. Remember, if you don't feel comfortable reading these terms out loud yet, that's part of why we're here. The more you familiarize yourself with this language and what it means, the more ready you will be to help your kids navigate their bodies in healthy ways.

Maybe some of you are blushing as you read these words. Maybe you feel like these words are inherently bad or crass. Remember, I'm not suggesting using "street language" or crude words for the body. When we think about it, all the nicknames we give to anatomy are actually quite strange. Using medical language highlights the reality of our bodies, invites us to treat them with seriousness while not avoiding them, and teaches children how to identify body parts. Further, as we mentioned earlier, it helps us equip children to identify abusive behavior and speak up about it with clarity and confidence. Let's explore in more detail why this is the case.

ANATOMICAL TERMS TO KNOW

MALE REPRODUCTIVE SYSTEM[1]

Purpose

- Produces and moves semen, the container for sperm
- Sends sperm into the female body during sexual intercourse
- Produces sex hormones, including testosterone

External Organs

There are internal and external organs, but we will focus on the external organs here.

- Penis: This organ includes the glans, the shaft, and the root. Its purpose is reproduction and urination.
    - *Glans: This is the tip or head of the penis. This is a where the urethra opening is. If a child is uncircumcised, the foreskin is the fold of skin that covers the glans. The glans is highly sensitive.*

- *Shaft: This is the largest portion of the penis and has layers of tissue that fill with blood when arousal occurs. The filling of the tissue with blood is what causes an erection.*
- *Root: This is the opposite end of the penis from the glans. The root connects the penis to the pelvic region.*

- Scrotum: This sac lies directly behind the root of the penis and holds a person's testicles. It protects the testicles and helps moderate temperature, since temperature can impact the production of sperm.
- Testicles: These are two egg-shaped structures within the scrotum. They are connected by the epididymis to a person's entire reproductive system. They produce sperm and testosterone.

ANATOMICAL TERMS TO KNOW

FEMALE REPRODUCTIVE SYSTEM

Purpose

- Provides entryway for sperm to enter the female body
- Protects genitalia inside the female body from infection
- Provides lubrication and pleasure during sexual intercourse

External Organs[2]

- Vulva: This is the most accurate term for the entire external genital region, including the mons pubis, labia majora, labia minora, and clitoris.
- Mons pubis: Also known as the pubic mound, this is a mound of tissue covering the pubic bone. It is divided into the labia majora and labia minora. This is the area that is covered with hair during puberty. It also releases pheromones through glands within it and impacts attraction.
- Labia majora: This large tissue offers protection to the organs in the external genital area. There are glands within it that provide lubrication when stimulated.

- Labia minora: This pink area is located inside the labia majora and can be found around the vaginal and urethral openings. The labia minora fills with blood when stimulated, which causes swelling and greater sensitivity.
- Clitoris: This is found in the upper end of the labia minora. It can become erect during sexual stimulation, much like the penis does. This is the area that, when stimulated, is extremely sensitive and can result in female orgasm, and its sole function is sexual pleasure.

Internal Organs[3]

- Vagina: This is the place in the birth canal where sperm enters and a baby exits the female body, connecting the external and internal genitalia. It is typically four to five inches long at full maturation. It is the place from which menstrual bleeding leaves the body.
- Uterus: The uterus is the pear-shaped area in the female body where the human embryo develops into a baby after fertilization. Its walls contract during labor, which is what helps move the baby out of the body through the cervix and vagina. If no baby is conceived during any given month, a woman's uterine lining, which has thickened throughout the menstrual cycle, sheds, which causes menstrual bleeding.
- Cervix: This is located in the lower region of a woman's uterus and becomes dilated during labor and delivery. It also is responsible for protecting against bacteria that could cause infection.
- Fallopian tubes: After the sperm enters the female body through the vaginal opening, cervix, and uterus, the sperm fertilizes the egg in one of these tubes. These are about four to five inches long.
- Ovaries: This is the area of the female body that is responsible for producing and releasing eggs each month as well as estrogen and progesterone and some male sex hormones. Each girl, at birth, has one million egg cells (oocytes). On average, about four hundred egg cells are released over the course of the life span.

ACCURATE LANGUAGE AND PROTECTING CHILDREN FROM ABUSE

Children who are taught accurate language may be more likely to tell a parent if someone tries to talk about their body or asks to see parts of their body, for at least two different reasons. First, using anatomical terms helps signal to children that they don't need to feel shame in discussing these body parts with their parents. If a child knows you are capable of talking about their bodies with them, and something happens to their body that makes them uncomfortable, they are much more likely to see you as an ally to talk to.

Second, using anatomical language is helpful for identifying cases where another person talks about a child's body and uses some sort of nickname. If a child comes home using language that wasn't taught in the home, this can signal to a parent that a child has encountered that language elsewhere. If you do hear language that differs from what you have taught a child, you can start by simply acknowledging, "That's a new word." Then you can calmly ask, "Where did you hear that word?"

Talking about sexual abuse is excruciating under any circumstances, so helping a kid know ahead of time what parts of the body could be violated will help with their overall sense of self-confidence and their ability to talk to you. We don't want a child believing that you can't handle this information, or believing they are protecting you from an uncomfortable conversation by keeping abuse a secret.[4]

IDENTIFYING ABNORMALITIES

Caleb was uncircumcised as a child. From about age two, his parents always spoke with him about his anatomy using medical language. He began to feel pain at the tip of his penis around the age of seven, and one night he told his dad and mom during bedtime prayers, "My penis hurts." Since they had also explained multiple times that he still had his foreskin due to their decision not to circumcise him as an infant, he knew to say, "Is my foreskin supposed to look red?" As it turned out, Caleb had a condition called phimosis, where the foreskin tightens and causes inflammation and pain. As an adult, Caleb later recalled that he wasn't afraid to talk about his concern with his parents, because it had always seemed so natural to talk about his body with them. He was able to get medical attention quickly because of his ability to be honest and talk openly with his parents.

There are many male- and female-specific complications or abnormalities that can occur during childhood. This is another reason it's so important to equip your child to understand their genitals enough to know when they are functioning well or poorly. Early identification and intervention are key, and you get to be part of the solution when you show your kids that they can count on you to help if things aren't quite right.

APPROPRIATE SETTINGS

You may be wondering, "When is a good time to talk with young kids about their bodies, and especially their genitalia?" Some of the most obvious moments happen at bath time, bedtime, or when a kid's diaper or clothing is being changed. These can be light moments when a child is relaxed, which is important so that they are open to conversation. They also allow you to set the framework for kids to understand who should assist them with these activities, and who should see their naked bodies or touch them near their genitals.

You don't need to say everything in one conversation, but sprinkling these comments throughout different times can help a child better understand their body and boundaries.

FOR BATH TIME

- "Baths are fun, aren't they? Baths are a time for you and Mommy [or Daddy] to play and talk after the day. You are naked because it's time to wash your body and scrub all the dirt away from the day. It's so good to be clean!"
- "Bath time is not something we do with people who aren't in our family. Our family rule is that only Mommy or Daddy give you a bath, unless one of us says otherwise. Your body is a beautiful gift from God. Let's get it all clean!"
- "Do you remember what we wash in the tub? We wash all the way from the tip of our head to the tips of our toes and everything in between! We need to make sure we wash your [vagina / penis / chest / arms / legs / face], too, so it stays clean."

FOR CHANGING CLOTHES

- "Alright, let's take your clothes off and get you ready for bedtime. Remember, you get naked because you are changing, and Mommy [or Daddy] is helping you with that. If someone else asks you to take off your clothes in front of them without Mommy [or Daddy], saying it's okay, do you know what you say? [Pause for answer.] That's right, you say no!"
- "If someone ever asks you to take your clothes off and tells you not to tell anyone because you will get in big trouble, that's not true. You'll never get in trouble for telling us the truth. In our family, we don't keep secrets from each other, remember? Surprises are great, but secrets are not."

FOR CHANGING DIAPERS

- "Let's go ahead and change your diaper. You peed, so it's time to wipe your vagina and clean around it. Doing that keeps your body clean and healthy. Your body is a gift from God, and this is a way to take good care of it."
- "It's time to change your diaper because you just pooped. We are going to wipe all around your butthole and around the shaft of your penis, because sometimes poop spreads all around. These wipes help keep everything clean, so you don't get a rash. Rashes hurt, so if you notice pain down there, tell me, and we have cream for that!"

Those are a lot of words to say, especially to an infant, aren't they! Saying this kind of thing early and often will be more for your sake at first than for your kid. It lets you practice getting comfortable with this language, so that by the time your child is old enough to really take in this language, there are very few (if any) signs of anxiety in you.

You may have older children and even teenagers whom you haven't had the opportunity to teach these simple lessons to yet, for any number of reasons. We'll discuss the appropriate settings to have these conversations with older kids in book 2, which will be about discussing sexuality with middle- and high-school kids. So hang tight—those tips are coming!

NOTICING AND MANAGING ANXIETY

Earlier I mentioned how important it is to have these conversations when your child is relaxed and more open. The same is true for you as a parent. If you have been running around all day, have barely had a second to breathe, and are rushing to get your kids in bed, this may not be the best time to bring up sexuality. The ideal would be to wait until you feel present, calm, and even playful.

For many parents, bath-time and bedtime routines can be stressful times of day. These moments often come at the end of a long day, feel rushed, and are the final tasks keeping you from a glass of wine or a sweet time with your partner. Putting in the hard work to enter into these moments calmly and playfully, at least sometimes, will make them more enjoyable and provide an opportunity for formative conversations with your child. Of course, this just isn't possible every night—don't beat yourself up for being human. But as often as you are able, finding ways to bring a spirit of calm and playfulness to these moments will help you create space for the conversations you are learning to have about the body.

TAKING CUES AND ANTICIPATING CURIOSITY

We've already talked about the importance of not overwhelming a child with information before they're ready for it. Let me give you an example. A client of mine shared with me that he has a strong aversion to talking with anyone about sex, even his wife. He shared that a major factor in his aversion was the fact that, when he was a child, his parents had extremely detailed conversations about their sex life at the dinner table. These conversations got even more vivid when his parents were drinking. He talked about how his parents had been terrified of "seeming prudish," and so they swung too far in the other direction. He remembered just how uncomfortable he felt in these moments. Now, as a parent of four young children, he was having a hard time understanding the value of explaining anatomy to his elementary-school kids, out of fear that he would "scandalize" them like he was scandalized as a kid.

It's valid to worry about overwhelming your child with more information than they are ready for—I'd encourage you to pay attention to the fear you feel in this area. In fact, one of the biggest concerns about incorporating sex education earlier in children's development is that it violates their innocence. This is an understandable concern, and it's appropriate for us to be cautious about exposing children to sexualized content in elementary school.

However, I want to make an important distinction between *sexualized* content and age-appropriate information about human *sexuality*. Teaching about genitalia is not necessarily a *sexualized* process. It would be sexualized, of course, if you were to do so in the context of showing a child pornographic images or videos that introduce the sexual function of these parts. But it doesn't have to be.

We want to find the balance between taking our cues from a child's questions and anticipating a child's curiosity. Some parents are willing to begin a conversation but aren't sure how much information to give once they've started. This is where taking a child's cues comes in. Start by saying less, then see how your child responds and go from there. For instance, let's imagine a child asks what their penis is for. Start by saying something like, "Your penis is the area of the body that helps you go to the bathroom. It's where pee comes out." There is no need to go into the reproductive aspect of male genitals right away, but make sure to keep the door open to further conversation. "We can talk about this more as you grow up. For now it's good to know that your penis is an important part of your body! That's why we take good care of it and keep it clean." (We'll look at more examples of this tactic in the next chapter.)

In addition to taking cues, there's also value in anticipating your child's curiosity. Some parents say that they'll wait to bring up sexuality until their child asks. However, many children never ask their parents about these topics without some prompting. These children might end up channeling their curiosity through pornography or explicit sexual content later in their development, often as a way to find answers to their questions, while feeling that they can't discuss these questions openly with their parents or other trusted adults. Anticipating a child's curiosity means bringing up brief conversations about these topics in order to signal your willingness to help them answer natural questions in real time.

I'd encourage you to teach your child about their genitalia just as you teach them about any other body part. Think of the song "Heads, Shoulders, Knees, and Toes." Picture how fun it is for kids to begin to learn about their bodies, and the sense of pride they can feel for knowing what these body parts are and what they are for.

Is it possible to make learning about genitalia neutral, and even something your child can be proud of? Let's find out.

CHAPTER 3

"WHAT IS HEALTHY EXPLORATION?"

TEACHING HEALTHY TOUCH

Touching genitalia and exploring genitalia through sensory play (that is, games like "doctor") is normal for kids. Many parents overreact to kids' exploration of their bodies, perhaps because of our own histories of unwanted sexual experiences or because we're afraid that our kids' behavior is unusual. In this chapter, I want to help you recognize the signs of healthy and unhealthy touch. Remember, we want to be always taking proactive steps to prevent abuse and neglect. Toward that end, we want to make the most of our children's natural curiosity by treating it as an opportunity to teach them about their bodies, honor their curiosity, and shape their behaviors in private and public settings.

AGE-APPROPRIATE CONVERSATIONS

One common concern I hear when I talk about these concepts is that parents do not want to prematurely unload information on their children. Preserving the innocence of children is essential and good. This is why we want to frame appropriate conversation topics by age range, so that you have confidence about what to say and when.

No matter your child's age, chapter 2 is for you. Remember that even with infants you can begin to practice using accurate terminology for genitalia. Accurate terminology may help you with managing any anxiety you have when talking about genitalia. It may also help you become more accustomed to the language, long before your child will remember the conversation. It doesn't mean you will teach them about every single word I listed in chapter 2, but it does mean that you will be clear about what each word means, so that when the time comes, you are ready to name what is there.

AGE-APPROPRIATE GUIDANCE

Ages 0–2

- Teaching Accurate Terms for Genitalia

Ages 2–5

- Teaching General Purposes of Genitalia
- Teaching about Privacy
- Teaching Setting-Appropriate Dress
- Setting Limits around Exploratory Play
- Distinguishing Exploratory Play from Concerning Sexual Touch

GETTING MORE SPECIFIC ABOUT GENITALIA

For ages zero to two, I recommend simply naming terms of external genitalia for a child (vulva, penis, anus). It's not necessary to go into the purposes of the genitalia at this point, but these early talks lay a foundation for future ones.

Between the ages of two and four, children notice their genitalia more specifically, and sometimes they start to notice differences between their own genitalia and others'. You may start to notice your child touching their genitals, playing with them, and being curious about them. Some kids will ask, "What is this thing between my legs?" Others will simply show their curiosity by touch and not be as direct about what they are thinking. Remain calm, especially when a child is doing normal things like touching their genitals. This will keep you from inadvertently shaming your child. After all, you wouldn't react negatively to a child touching their arm or eyeball or pinky toe. While not all body parts have the same function, they are all good, they all have a purpose, and they are all worth learning about.

This is the age when kids can start to learn the role of different body parts. Most kids don't only want to know "what"; they also want to know "why." Why is *that* there?

If your child asks you about a body part when you don't have time to answer, or you simply can't remember the purpose of any given body part, that's no problem! You can tell your child that you will let them know another time. If you need, you can look back at chapter 2's list of genitalia names and functions. Remember to keep your explanations simple at first, and tell your child they can always ask more questions if they want.

OBSERVING SELF

One of the useful concepts I teach in therapy is called "the observing self." The goal is to grow our ability to "notice" what is happening to and around us with curiosity rather than reactivity. Let's go back to the moment when a mom spotted her child touching his penis. Out of reactivity, she could do any number of things, from slapping his hand away to saying, "Gross! Don't touch that!" If she reacts like this, it may be a good indicator that she needs to slow down, take a few deep breaths, and circle back to the conversation later. She could begin by saying, "I'm sorry I yelled at you earlier. That wasn't okay for me to yell like that. I'm not disgusted by you."

But what if we could catch these moments even sooner? What if we could slow down to the point where we begin observing ourselves the moment we see our child touching their private parts? We can notice what is happening and notice the reaction it brings up in us. Then we can say to ourselves, "I am noticing they are touching their privates, and I am noticing my reaction is _____. I am going to take a few deep breaths now. I am going to wait; this is not urgent. If I am still upset, I am going to walk away for a minute to catch my breath. If I am calmer, I can calmly say, 'Honey, I notice you touching your ____. Do you remember how we talked about that?'"

Beginning your words to your child with a question is so helpful because it lets you know if your child is actually learning or if they haven't quite understood what you are trying to teach. It also makes the moment into a conversation instead of a lecture. If your child says they don't remember what you've talked about, say it again: "We talked about how certain parts of the body are so important that we keep them clean and protected. We put clothes on them, and we touch them mainly when we are cleaning them. These are private parts. Do you remember which parts of your body are private parts? [Pause for answer.] Good job!"

Later in the same conversation, or in another conversation later that day, you could add, "Okay, we do not touch these parts in front of other people, even when we are really curious about them and why they are there. Do you have any questions about your ____ that you were touching? That's normal, because sometimes we touch things when we want to know them better. Still, we don't touch them unless it's time to take a bath or wash them after going to the bathroom, remember?"

EXPLAINING ABOUT PRIVACY

Age two is also when you can begin to explain concepts like privacy. Privacy is "the ability of an individual or group to seclude themselves or information about themselves, and thereby express themselves selectively."[1] Children, like adults, need to know that there are aspects of our personhood that should only be unveiled with our permission. This is key. We want to teach kids that no one has a right to their bodies without their permission, even when visiting a doctor.

Another definition of privacy is "the state of being free from public attention."[2] This definition can help us understand how to begin teaching children about privacy. I want children to expect moments when they don't need to perform for others and when they know that their bodies won't be on public display. There are spaces and places where they can expect not to be disturbed by others, and these are the spaces where they can feel the freedom to undress safely. At the same time, children need to be taught that there are spaces where privacy isn't available, and covering their bodies is important in these spaces. Giving your child "disturbance-free spaces" actually helps them learn the difference between public and private space, which helps them learn which behaviors should be saved for privacy.

Let's think together about your response if your child was to ask, "Why do I need to wear clothes in public or when family friends are over for dinner?" For younger children, we can keep it simple. "Public places are places where strangers are. There are certain things that we do in our home that we don't do outside of our home." Then you can give examples of this: "What are things we do in our home that we don't do outside of it? We go in the fridge and get food when we are hungry without asking, but we wouldn't do that in someone else's home. We take a bath in our home, but we wouldn't take a bath in the home of someone we don't know. We can build a fort in our home, but we wouldn't go do that in a grocery store."

After laying this foundation, you can continue: "There are also certain things we do in front of people and certain things we do without people watching." With a child who is a bit older and more verbally engaged, you could ask them to tell you examples themselves: "Can you think of things we do in front of people and things we do without people watching?" Have examples handy. You could say something like, "In front of people, we play games, wash our hands, and sing. There are things we wouldn't do with people watching (except for parents) like going to the bathroom, changing our clothes, or taking a shower. Can you think of any other examples?"

PRIVACY AND SOCIAL MEDIA

While an entire chapter, chapter 10, will be dedicated to technology and your child, I can't talk about privacy without acknowledging the way social media impacts this conversation. I want you to imagine, as an adult, walking down the street and noticing someone is taking your picture. How would that feel for you? Now imagine the person posts it without your permission on their social media account with thousands of followers. What would that be like for you?

If you are honest, you may feel exposed, scared, tense, uncomfortable, angry, and violated. Why is that? Perhaps because, on a fundamental level, we have a sense that we ought to be the gatekeeper of our own being. We don't want our image, our body, or our personhood to be used for someone else's gain, and especially not without our giving the "okay."

This is worth reflecting on as we think about our own social media use and what we post about our children, and especially about their bodies.

Some people refuse to post photos of their child's face on social media. Others draw the line at refusing to show their children unclothed. Others are unwilling to post photos of their children in a bathing suit. Others will post photos of their children naked, in a bathtub, and so on. I am not here to prescribe a one-size-fits-all approach, as if there is a single clear answer for every parent. What I hope to do is give you time to pause and think about how privacy relates to your children or children in your care. Does the way we use our social media give our children the opportunity to experience privacy and learn about spaces that are free from the observation of others? If no, what would it look like to change our social media use in a way that gave our children more ownership and understanding of their privacy?

Again, I will weigh in more on how to engage wisely with technology use that involves your children in chapter 10, but it's worth naming now that we want to be consistent with kids in what we are teaching them about privacy. This might mean letting your child have a say in what you post online, encouraging them to say what they are comfortable with and what they are not. It could also involve asking yourself whether you as an adult would want an image like that of you as a young child somewhere on the internet. These conversations can be helpful guides for you as you make decisions about social media use on behalf of your (or other people's) children.

SETTING-APPROPRIATE DRESS

Yet another building block for healthy conversation about privacy is helping kids identify when and where nakedness is expected and acceptable and when and where clothing is appropriate. This approach to privacy doesn't devalue the body. Rather, it expresses the value of each human person uniquely and recognizes that people don't always have a right to observe us. We know this intuitively; some of us have experienced the terrible violation of being watched by another person without our permission. Recognizing how we feel when we're being observed without permission can help us understand how important it is not to be observed at all times. Privacy goes hand in hand with teaching children about setting-appropriate dress and nakedness.

As you talk with a child about setting-appropriate dress, keep in mind what you do and don't want them to think about *why* it's best to cover up. Unfortunately, it's all too common for young children (especially girls) to hear messages about modesty that tell them their body is dangerous to others and their sexual organs put them at risk of harm. Young children have sometimes walked away with the sense that, if they were harmed, it would be their fault. Knowing what messages we *don't* want to send to a child (that their body is bad, dirty, or merely a temptation to others) can help us discover the messages we *do* want to send about privacy and nakedness.

So let's get practical. Imagine a naked four-year-old boy running onto a back porch at a large gathering at his family's home. Guests start to laugh—some out of discomfort, others because they think it is cute and harmless. The dad gets up to take the child inside to get dressed. Even in this simple moment, the dad's response to his child is so important.

Dad could respond in a lot of different ways. He could yell at his son, saying things like, "You embarrassed me! Don't ever do that again." He could spank his son, punishing him for not knowing the appropriate dress for the moment. Though some of you may have responded in this way to your kids in the past, these aren't the responses I would recommend.

Here's an approach that might be more helpful. Calmly, Dad can get up and walk over to his little boy. Still calmly, but also with a serious tone, he can say, "We wear clothes at family gatherings. We don't run around without clothes on. Let's go get you dressed." Once inside, Dad can reiterate what he said outside. The repetition is important because children can often miss their parents' messages in moments of discomfort, playfulness, or distraction. Setting limits, gently, is so critical at this age. However, we don't want to punish children for not immediately understanding things that their brains are still learning to understand. Just like we wouldn't expect a child to do algebra in pre-K, we can't expect a child to navigate setting-appropriate dress flawlessly. The same could be said for boundaries around exploratory play, which we'll tackle next.

UNDERSTANDING EXPLORATORY PLAY

Exploratory play is when a child incorporates their bodies, and sensory experiences like touch, into their play. This frees a child up to make sense of their experiences and understand in new ways. This usually begins in the first few months of life and continues through age five.[3] One obvious way this happens, as it relates to genitalia, is when a little girl begins to rub her vaginal area, noticing the pleasure it gives her, or a little boy begins to notice his penis and touch it or move it around.

It's important to set boundaries around exploratory play with genitalia, even while we recognize that this exploratory play is normal in early child development. Talking about these boundaries is even more important when you have neighbors and older siblings around your elementary-school-aged child. You might begin easing into these conversations with a three-year-old who is around older children or in settings like a daycare where they will not have your oversight, or you can tweak the language for older kids as well.

Three is also the typical age when children begin to play games like "doctor," when brothers begin to compare their penises and comment on them, and when children at playdates may undress together or show their genitals to one another. Each of these moments requires intervention from parents and caregivers—but as always, the way you intervene matters.

Time and time again in therapy sessions, clients have shared with me their memories of early exploratory play. Many feared that such play made them "a monster," "sick," or "a predator." When we talked more about where these feelings came from, it became clear that their caregivers had responded to their exploratory play out of fear, reinforcing the idea that these children were "bad" for engaging with their bodies or the bodies of others in these exploratory ways. If you scream at a child, saying things like, "What is wrong with you?" or "Stop that right now! That's disgusting," that child is likely to hear, "I am bad," "I am disgusting." These messages had attached themselves to my clients at a young age and persisted into adulthood.

I want to make it clear that I'm not suggesting parents should ignore their child's behavior just because it's normal. It's normal for a child to throw food in their high chair, but to help them develop appropriately, you'll teach them not to do that. What I am saying is that the way you teach your child matters. You can respond to developmentally appropriate behavior in a way that helps your children grow out of it, while still not shaming them for behaving in developmentally appropriate ways.

Ralph came into therapy and shared that he walked in on his three-year-old and five-year-old boys "playing doctor," with the older boy touching the naked younger boy's penis. "I freaked out!" Ralph said sheepishly. "I slapped my five-year-old's hand away from his younger brother and told them to never do that again. I could tell they were shocked and uncomfortable, and they both started to cry. I have no idea how to talk about this with them, and they will probably forget about it. I am just hoping it doesn't happen again."

Maybe you can relate to Ralph's dilemma. He's right that this behavior might not happen again, at least not any time soon. But his response may have also sent the message to his sons that their sexuality or a particular body part is shameful, scary, and bad. If they internalize these beliefs, they may be more likely later to find ways to secretly channel their sexual desire through things like pornography or masturbation. Because they've learned that sexual interest shouldn't be expressed openly in front of their parents, it becomes more easily tied to secrecy and hiddenness.

As parents who want to raise sexually whole future adults, then, behavior reduction can't be our only goal. We want to help our children grow into adults who refrain from compulsive behaviors out of a sense that they deserve better, not out of a sense that they would be punished or shamed if someone knew the truth of what was happening behind closed doors.

Another result of Ralph's response to his kids might be that this kind of behavior *will* happen again, but in a more hidden and covert way. Ralph's older son may remember the rush of energy he got at being caught touching his brother's penis. He may look for other opportunities to do so, not fully realizing why. He may become drawn to the secrecy of it, leading to compulsive sexual behaviors later, or he may go looking for more opportunities to engage in secret exploratory play now.

Instead of hoping it doesn't happen again, Ralph would be better off having a follow-up conversation with his kids. He could start the talk this way: "Hey, boys, can I talk to you for a minute? Remember when I screamed at you the other day for playing doctor?"

It's worth noting that some kids will say they don't remember. That's okay—Ralph can just keep going. "Well, I did, and I lost my temper. Screaming at you like that was not okay." Looking directly at the older brother, he can say, "I am sorry for slapping your hand," and to the younger brother he can say, "I didn't handle that right. In the future I am going to work to stay calm in those moments."

Once Ralph has apologized, he can teach his kids next: "It's normal to want to play games like doctor. And real doctors do check our penises to make sure they are clean and working right, so it makes sense that you wanted to do that too. I also notice you are both very curious about your penises and noticing them more. That also makes sense! But because we aren't real doctors, we don't do everything real doctors do. When you play doctor, you can touch any parts of the body that aren't covered by bathing suits. So it's okay to touch each other's arms, legs, feet, nose, mouth, eyes, and ears, as long as you have permission. But we don't touch each other's private parts, even with their permission, because only real doctors do that, and only when your mom or me is around. And if someone asks us to stop playing doctor, we respect that and stop. What questions do you have about this?"

If there aren't any questions, Ralph can end by saying, "I am grateful that this happened the other day, even though I didn't handle it right in the moment. I want us to be able to talk about your growing bodies, especially if you have questions about them. When you have questions, I hope we can talk about it more."

I want to also think through an example of exploratory play between children who are not siblings. These situations often evoke an even stronger response from caregivers and can be a bit more complicated to navigate.

Picture this scenario. Two families are having a dinner get-together. They have two children each; one family has two girls, and the other has two boys. The kids are ages five and three in both families, making for a natural playdate after dinner. While the parents are lost in good conversation, the kids move into a back bedroom in the house to play. As one of the parents goes back that way to use the bathroom, he overhears one of his boys say, "Time to play 'take off your pants'!" He immediately returns to his wife and the other couple and tells them what he heard. All four parents walk to the back room to intervene.

Trying to stay as calm as possible, they ask, "What are you doing?" The giggling kids reply, "Playing!" The first dad says, "I heard you say you were playing a game about taking off your pants?" The kids giggle more, bouncing around and screaming, "Yes! We are being silly."

How would you respond in this situation? The best thing to do right in that moment is to set limits calmly and clearly. "There are lots of games you can play with your friends. Taking off your pants is not one of them. Even though that feels silly to you, it is not a game, and it is not okay to do with friends. Your private parts are private, which means you don't show them to others, and you don't ask others to show theirs. Those are the rules of our family, okay?"

Some parents may be concerned about the way their kids respond in that moment. They may continue laughing, insisting they are just being silly and ignoring the redirection. When kids act silly and goofy in those moments, it can be a sign of their own discomfort. They are trying to signal that everything is okay because they are feeling nervous or uncomfortable. This is a common deflection technique—we do it as adults anytime we make a joke when we feel uncomfortable.

If a child is using defense mechanisms like this, it can be hard for them to incorporate new information and learn. It is essential to have important conversations when a child is relatively calm. This may mean saying, "I notice you are giggling right now. Sometimes we giggle when we feel unsure or uncomfortable or even nervous. Let's wait to talk more about this when you are calmer."

In a follow-up conversation, with a casual and curious tone, you can circle back to the conversation. Start by asking a general question about the night: "What was your favorite part of last night? What about your least favorite part?" After you hear a bit about the night overall, bring up that moment. Say as casually as possible, "You all made a game out of pulling down your pants. I want to talk about that more." You can first ask another question, continuing to show curiosity rather than criticism or anxiety. "What was it like to play that way?" Some kids may say that they felt uncomfortable or felt the game was wrong or bad. Others may say that they thought it was fun, silly, shocking, or interesting. They may say something like, "I've never seen a [penis/vagina] before." No matter what they say, validate their perspective. A validation phrase usually goes like this: "It makes sense that you thought/felt ____." This doesn't mean you agree with your child's experience or want to reinforce the behavior. It simply means you see your child where they are.

If you can't validate their experience because you don't yet understand, it is okay to ask a follow-up question after summarizing what they said last. You might say something like, "Oh, you thought it was fun and silly. What about it was fun and silly?" They may say, "It tickled when my friend touched my butt with his hand." This is where you validate, "Oh, it tickled! It makes sense that you would think that was fun and silly, because tickling can be really fun and silly sometimes, can't it?" This kind of understanding response helps to keeps a child (or, frankly, any one of us) from becoming guarded. When we feel understood and seen, we tend to open up more. A child may say, "Yeah, but it also felt weird," in which case you can also validate that it felt both fun and weird at the same time.

Then you can use the moment to teach something of value: "I want to remind you that, in our family, one of our rules is that we do not show our private parts to others, and we don't ask to see others' private parts. Even if it feels silly or fun or if you are curious, it is important to remember our family rules and respect those. They are rules that help keep you and your friends safe when you play. Just like we have rules about touching a hot stove or staying on the sidewalk, we have rules about touch. What questions do you have about that?"

A final piece of the puzzle here is talking with the other couple about this. Much in the same way as you did with your child, you want to communicate the following:

- "We have a family rule where we do not show private parts to others and don't ask to see others' private parts."
- "We expect our kids to honor those rules."
- "Would you be willing to discuss this with your kids, too?"

DISCUSSING EXPLORATORY PLAY

Here are the steps for discussing exploratory play with your child: (1) Be calm and be curious. Remember, this is not an emergency. (2) Ask general questions about the day. (3) Ask specifically about the exploratory play. (4) Ask what it was like for them to engage in that play. (5) Validate what your child was thinking and feeling and the context for their behavior. (6) Reassert limits.

Too often, parents go immediately into lecture mode. I see this happen all the time as a therapist, and I watch a child disconnect from the moment, tune out, or retaliate without ever listening. This is a valuable opportunity for parents to model active listening, a skill we want to teach children. The mantra "Listen first, then listen some more, then speak" will go further with your child than any lecture ever could.

Some adults may worry about a child thinking they are angry when they are having these conversations, even if they aren't actually angry. Let's think about how parents can respond if a child worries the parent is angry. Since kids are learning about how emotions show up in our faces, they may need a bit of coaching on this piece. They may ask, "Why are you mad, Mom/Dad?" Calmly and clearly respond, "What about my face looks mad, honey?" Let the child answer. As they do that, again validate: "Oh, I can see how you would wonder that." Then reflect your reality. "Actually, my face is serious. It may look mad, but serious is not the same thing as mad. It's actually just a serious face because I care about you, and this is an important conversation for us to have. Your safety is very important to me."

However, if you are angry in the moment, don't deny it. That can be very frustrating for a child! Surely many of us have experienced a time when someone screamed at us and we asked, "Why are you mad?" and they flatly denied it. It does no good to disavow what you are feeling. If you are angry, be prepared to acknowledge it: "You are right! I do look angry, because sometimes I feel anger when I get scared that something could hurt you. I want to protect you, and I feel angry when I can't do it perfectly. And people touching your private parts can be hurtful in the long run, so I want to help you protect yourself. I'm not angry at you, but I do feel anger about what happened to you." If you are feeling anger to the point that you are yelling or raising your voice, that is a cue that now is not the right time for this talk. So if you are feeling this way, tell your child, "I am feeling a lot right now, and I want to talk about this when I can do it calmly. I am going to take a break, and we can talk about this later." All of this is excellent modeling. Don't be afraid when your emotions are at the surface. Take their cue, and take a step back when you need to.

Explaining that you are angry because you worry about a child being hurt may lead a curious child to ask an understandable follow-up question. "What will happen if we let someone touch our butt/vagina/penis? Why can't we play that way? It was fun. It tickled." Kids say very blunt things sometimes, don't they? When you zoom out, though, it's a great question. Repeat back their question first, and say what a great question it is. This both encourages your child to ask you more questions and also buys you time to answer calmly! "What a great question. I am glad you asked. And your question is, What happens if we let someone touch us there? Why can't we do it if it was fun and tickled?" Then take time to respond:

> "Some types of touch feel good as a kid and are good for us. Other types of touch feel good as a kid, and they are still not good for us. A hug can feel good and, with people we are close to, is good for us. Or when Mom or Dad plays with your hair or rubs your back, it can feel good, and it is good for you. Having someone else touch your private parts can feel good, even at times when it isn't good. It's okay for us to touch our privates when cleaning or moving them to be comfortable, but not for others to touch as a game.
>
> "Your private parts are meant for important things. That's why we keep them clean and protect them from harm. Sometimes things that feel good to our private parts can hurt our heart later. It can make our heart feel sad. Mom and Dad's job is to help you do things that help your heart and don't hurt it. So that's why we want to teach you this, okay?"

The most important thing about these conversations is keeping lines of communication open. We do not want a child to retreat from talking to us about these important situations. You get to lay a foundation for your future conversations with your child, no matter how poorly you feel you may have handled these conversations in the past.

WHEN TOUCH OF PRIVATE AREAS IS A RED FLAG

Are there ever times when we ought to be concerned about exploratory play and touch of private areas? Is it truly always normal for one kid to touch their or another kid's private areas? This is a critical question. Thankfully, there are reliable guides for answering it.[4] We will address self-stimulation, also known as masturbation, more explicitly in book 2. For now, as we focus on younger children, the important thing is to understand how to identify red flags in this area.

First of all, when in doubt, ask a trusted source. Even when you feel sure, ask a trusted source. Do not rely on yourself alone to discern this question. If you are concerned, and especially when your child seems uncomfortable with something, bring it to a doctor or mental health professional to get guidance.

One variable to consider when it comes to touch between children that involves genitalia or breasts is the age range of the children involved. If there is a four-year age gap or more between children, they are no longer peers. Sexual touch in those circumstances is a serious red flag. This is not a black-and-white issue, so if a child feels uncomfortable with an older child's touch, even if there isn't a four-year age gap, trusted adults ought to take action. This comes into play especially in larger families, families where children are more spread out in age, and blended families.

First, let's think about boundaries around sexual touch and exposure in the context of age differences. While it may be appropriate for a two-year-old and four-year-old to take a bath together, it would not be okay for a four-year-old and nine-year-old to take a bath together unclothed. While they could wear bathing suits in the tub, like they do in a pool, expecting children to be comfortable with being undressed in the tub together at these ages is a mistake. This is because, as children get older, they gain different perspectives on modesty and privacy, and greater self-awareness emerges. This means an older child will typically feel uncomfortable undressing or bathing in front of or with a younger child. Teaching children the importance of privacy even before their self-awareness drives them to request it is key. You can set the framework for this by fostering in your child a sense of awareness of the different developmental levels of your children of various ages, or of cousins and close friends.

The American Academy of Pediatrics (AAP) offered a clinical report in 2009 that gives some insight into which behaviors are common (and usually easily redirected) and which behaviors are uncommon (and often more difficult to correct and typically cause for more concern) in children aged two to six. The information isn't necessarily a way of diagnosing sexual abuse in children, but it can help parents know which behaviors are red flags and should be given further attention.[5] Common behaviors, listed below, are infrequent, and a child can be distracted from doing them and will stop when told to:

- Touching genitals in private or public
- Viewing or touching peers' or siblings' genitals
- Showing genitals to a peer
- Standing or sitting too close to another person
- Attempting to view another person naked (peer or adult)

Beyond these, some behaviors are less common, but still considered within the range of what might sometimes happen. These less common behaviors, can take a few times to redirect in some children, but we expect a child to adjust behavior after several efforts to calmly set limits around this. When these behaviors happen, I'd encourage parents to look into whether norms around nakedness in the home need to be addressed, as well as to consider whether there are any concerning factors in the childcare situation, possible exposure to pornography, and so on. Remain calm in redirecting these behaviors, and seek support from a mental health professional if you have questions about how to intervene if these behaviors do not stop after several attempts to redirect.

These less common behaviors include the following:

- Rubbing the body against others
- Trying to insert their tongue in the mouth of another while kissing
- Touching adult genitals

Behaviors that the AAP describes as uncommon are concerning if they are persistent and resistant to distraction or intervention from others. These are signs that a child may be experiencing situational factors such as violence, abuse, or neglect. These uncommon behaviors may include the following:

- Asking someone to engage in a specific sexual act
- Inserting objects into genitals
- Explicitly imitating sexual intercourse
- Touching the genital area of an animal

Finally, the sexual behaviors that are even less common and cause for greater concern are those that must be reported to Child Protective Services whenever possible. Examples of these very uncommon behaviors include the following:

- Sexual behaviors between children where there is a four-year age gap or more
- Displaying sexual behaviors daily
- Engaging in sexual behaviors that result in emotional distress or physical pain for another person
- Sexual behaviors that incorporate physical aggression
- Sexual behaviors that are coercive

These are behaviors that a child continually goes back to even after being told not to.

We will address in chapter 7 how to handle moments when you observe concerning sexual behaviors. For now, I simply want to help you distinguish normal body exploration (for two- to six-year-olds) from concerning sexual behaviors. You can expect the common behaviors to gradually develop and to recede as a child gets older, unless there are developmental factors impacting this. Understanding what behavior is normal enables you to know if there are ever any urgent red flags to respond to.

SETTING LIMITS AROUND TOUCH IN PUBLIC

If a child has ongoing difficulties with the command to refrain from touching their private parts, here are some tips:

- It is good to come up with some helpful cues to remind a child to stop touching themselves. The key word here is "helpful." The best cue will be one that you and your child come up with together. You could ask them, "What could I say to help you remember that you need to stop touching your private parts?" Some parents come up with a quick distraction phrase or activity like, "Show me your hands!" or "Point to five things you can see!"

- Offer a hug or another form of physical touch that can be a comfort. This is especially useful if it seems as if a child's desire to touch their genitals is primarily about managing anxiety and soothing themselves. This is not concerning in and of itself, and you want to teach your kids alternative ways to soothe themselves in public and private.
- If distraction and soothing do not seem to help, it can be useful to find a time to sit down with your child (again, make sure to do this when you and they are calm and feeling neutral) and ask them about it. You can say something like, "I notice it is often difficult to keep from touching your ____. Do you notice that?"
- Then be curious about what the behavior is doing for your child. What makes them turn to it even when it leads to redirection? "How does it help to touch yourself?" "What do you like about touching yourself there?" "What might be making it hard to stop?"
- Only after being curious about what this behavior is doing for them can we move to problem-solving. This is where you can say, "What can we do to help you with that? It doesn't seem like what we are doing so far is working. Any ideas?"

Notice my language is centered around "we." This keeps you from shaming and blaming language and tone. Statements like "You always do that" and "You never listen" are overgeneralizations that will make any of us, including a child, defensive.

PATIENCE, PATIENCE, PATIENCE

One last thing for now. Before you get upset that your child is again playing with their private parts after what feels like the one thousandth time you have asked them not to, think about any of the habits you have formed in your life. Maybe you used to bite your nails, crack your knuckles, or pick your nose. (Or maybe you still do.) Has yelling you into submission ever helped? Sometimes kids engage in their habitual behaviors reactively (especially when they are trying to manage stress by doing so). Keep this in mind so that you can offer patience in the moments when it feels as if you just told them to stop a behavior and they are doing it again.

As we bring this chapter to a close, you have a better foundation for identifying healthy and unhealthy touch, explaining privacy, and being age-appropriate in how you introduce a child to different concepts. Next, we want to look together at expectations around touch between children and adults. Should you expect a child to hug you when you greet them or sit on your lap because you ask them to? Is it rude for a child to say no? That's what we will tackle next.

CHAPTER 4

"SHOULD I MAKE THEM HUG STRANGERS?"

ANSWERING QUESTIONS ABOUT PHYSICAL TOUCH WITH OTHERS

This chapter addresses the most common question I hear from parents: "Is a child being impolite if they don't hug Aunt Kathy when she comes over for Christmas?"

I want to start by explaining why it's best never to force a child to show physical affection, particularly with extended family members. The pressure we might feel to be "polite" by forcing physical affection can teach children that it is rude to speak up when something happens that they feel uncomfortable with. What I want for children is to know that it is never rude to set a boundary. It is actually an enormous act of justice to do so, especially when it means protecting oneself and others.

Of course, there may be cultural practices in some families that add a layer of complexity to the conversation about expectations around physical touch. For example, in some families, adult family members may commonly kiss a child's forehead when they greet them, and receiving this kiss could be a sign of respect.[1] These cultural dynamics are important for families to work through in a way that respects both your children and your culture.

Most of the sexual abuse of children involves someone the child already knows in some capacity. With that in mind, this chapter will outline how to set boundaries around physical touch with those a child knows, including siblings. We'll discuss how parents sometimes communicate to their children that certain groups of people (such as priests and pastors, parents, extended family, and siblings) can always be trusted. This messaging can perpetuate the silence of abuse because children are trained not to question their abuser. This is why I want to move you toward building open communication with your children about boundaries around physical touch with others as early and often as possible.

ISN'T IT RUDE?

I remember teaching a class to a group of Christian therapists in training. A dad of four raised his hand and asked a version of the question that kicks off this chapter: "Isn't it rude to let your kids reject a hug from family? I get it with strangers, but these are people I care about. I don't want to teach my kids that it's okay to be rude."

I asked him a bit more to understand his concern about being seen as rude. He talked about how some family members only get to see his children a few times a year. He talked about how hurtful it can be to others and how awkward it can feel for him if a family member reaches out for a hug and a kid cowers away. And he is right. It can feel awkward to witness that moment. It can feel awkward not knowing how to respond, especially when the family member is visibly upset by the interaction. But enduring these awkward moments and responding appropriately is doable. More than that, it is worth it if it helps your child in the long run. Therein lies the fundamental question: *Does it help or hurt your child to allow them to refrain from physical touch in these moments?*

To answer this dad's question—and hopefully yours, too—I want to share three stories that illustrate how teaching your child that they do not owe people physical touch helps protect them. These stories deal with the reality of sexual trauma, so take your time as you move through them.

I learned all three of these stories sitting in a room full of survivors of childhood sexual abuse. Though I was the one facilitating the group therapy session, they had so much wisdom to offer me when it came to how best to protect children. As we discussed the factors that they believe had put them at risk for abuse, they repeatedly gave an answer that may surprise you:

Politeness. Again and again, they agreed. Politeness was one of the contributors to their abuse.

WHEN POLITENESS MATTERS MORE THAN SAFETY

Here are the stories that three clients shared as they talked about the danger of politeness:

> "My mom was really worried about what others would think of her and her children if they weren't polite. As a single parent, she already felt like she was being judged at family gatherings. She always told us to smile and accept any forms of affection people wanted to give. She would remind us that we only saw some of our extended family members once every few years, so we needed to make the time count and let them know how much we loved them. Little did she know that one of my uncles was capitalizing on those irregular visits to molest me, and I never knew that loving him could mean saying no to his advances. I didn't want to be rude or get in trouble for not being polite. I still haven't told my mom that this ever happened."
>
> "I was so uncomfortable around my abuser, an older child in a family whose parents were my dad's best friends, that I would hide under a table every time we were going to events she would be at. I got screamed at for making us late and was told that if I kept making us late, I was going to be grounded, because I needed to learn how insulting it was to others to keep them waiting. I was six and didn't know how to talk about what was waiting for me at those events, and why I did not want to go. I didn't end up telling my parents until I was about fifteen, and they didn't believe me at first because it took so long for me to decide to share."
>
> "My dad always stressed that they were family. We can trust family, he said. No one told me that sometimes we actually can't always trust family. So, I didn't know what to do when my grandpa proved untrustworthy when he would give me baths. It took everything for me to tell someone, and

> it wasn't until I was in my late twenties that I finally decided to tell my parents."

These stories are difficult to write and equally difficult to read. Imagine living through them. Perhaps some of you have had experiences like these and know how difficult it is to live through the nightmare of sexual trauma. Abuse is a fundamental attack on the safety, security, and innocence of a child. It is tragic in countless ways. What's even more tragic is when we fail to protect against it because we are prioritizing politeness over safety.

LEARNING BOUNDARY-SETTING FOR THE FUTURE

To understand the significance and value of teaching children that it's okay to be uncomfortable with other people's physical touch, think of your life as an adult—especially if you are a woman. Imagine that you are walking to the bathroom in a restaurant during a work event, and your boss reaches out his hand and smacks your butt as you walk by him. Or perhaps he comes up behind you at work and begins to massage your shoulders. Is it rude to say no to that physical touch? Is it rude to smack away his hand? Is it rude to tell someone what he did?

If adults are right to speak up when we are uncomfortable and to say no to physical affection that makes us uncomfortable, how much more is this true for children? If we know it is hard for many adults to speak up in these tenuous and stressful moments, how much more so for children? Adults who struggle to stand up for themselves in the case of unwanted advances will struggle even more if they were taught as children that doing so is rude or impolite.

As we think critically about the narrative that it is impolite for a child to say no to physical touch, its logic begins to crumble. In fact, it's wildly inappropriate to expect a four-year-old who has never met a person, or who barely remembers them, to want to be physically close to that person without knowing anything about them. We would never do this as adults—why do we demand it of kids?

If we teach children to ignore their gut when it comes to receiving physical touch as children, it will be harder for them to learn to listen to their gut as adults. Telling a child who withdraws from an adult whom they don't know well that they must override their gut feeling for the sake of perceived politeness only further perpetuates this problem.

IF IT'S NOT RUDE, WHAT IS IT?

Teaching a child involves not only telling them what not to do, but also helping them learn what to do. Children who turn down physical touch could be accused of being rude. This is as true when they are kids as when they are adults. How do we prepare kids for these types of perceptions, giving them a positive vision of how to respond and what it means to respond differently? While the next chapter will deal more explicitly with how children say no, I want to focus in this chapter on the broad concepts that drive their response.

If it's not rude to decline physical touch, what is it?

I see it first and foremost as a boundary. Boundaries are essential in every human relationship, and a lack of boundaries can cause real havoc in our lives.

Setting a boundary is, at its core, also a pathway to growing in virtue. What is the virtue to be discovered within setting a boundary? Justice. Justice, simply put, is giving to each person what is due them. We often think of this in the context of giving *others* their due. Another aspect of justice is actually giving to *ourselves* what is due, which includes allowing ourselves to set and keep the boundaries that will protect us and keep us safe from avoidable harm. It can also include setting boundaries that keep us from giving to others what is *not* their due, such as free access to our body. Not only that, but boundaries help us cultivate healthy relationships. They don't just keep out the bad in relationships, but they also create the space for the good, true, and beautiful in our relational world.

Now back to physical touch. When a child declines physical touch they are uncomfortable with, we can reinforce this by celebrating the justice within even that seemingly small act. They are taking care of themselves in a big way, and it's important for a child to know that!

There are so many things that we can't prepare a child for in life, because so much of it is unexpected. But there are some moments we all know will happen, and I want to help you prepare your kids for them proactively as often as possible.

Let's do that more now. Imagine Aunt Kathy, whom your family hasn't seen in years, is driving through your area and coming for dinner. She has never met any of your children, who are five, three, and eighteen months old. Before she comes, you prep your children, explaining the ways to be hospitable and warm. You say, "You are not expected to hug her, even when she is leaving, but you can do something you feel comfortable with to greet her. You could say hi, wave, or smile, because you don't know her yet, even though Mom knows her. So you do not have to hug her, even if she asks. You have a right to your space, and your body is not for other people to touch just because they want to. You can hug Aunt Kathy if you want to, but you don't have to, okay?"

Now let's imagine Aunt Kathy does in fact ask for a hug. And let's imagine your five-year-old, Mary Grace, who is quite feisty, shakes her head and says, "No, I don't have to hug you because my body is not for touching." Aunt Kathy is shocked! She is from a generation where that would have been rude.

If you can, I'd advise that you speak up immediately. This keeps Aunt Kathy from saying something guilt-inducing to Mary Grace. You could say something like, "That's right, Mary Grace! Good memory. Our bodies aren't just for touching. You can smile or wave or something else to Aunt Kathy, but you don't have to hug her if you aren't ready for that." Before bed that night, be sure to circle back and celebrate your child's direct response. "I am so proud of you. You are getting so good at speaking up for yourself! You did a great job tonight when Aunt Kathy asked for a hug. It isn't always easy to speak up for ourselves, but you did it! Your body isn't there for others to touch, and you stood up for that! That is the right thing to do. It's okay to hug if you want to, but you don't have to."

After the fact, you could circle back and let Aunt Kathy know in a text message or call, "Thanks again for the visit! I know it can be shocking when kids turn down a hug. I hope you know it wasn't personal. We teach our kids that it is okay for them not to hug if they aren't comfortable with someone yet, and we give them other options so they can still be polite. We loved having you and can't wait for your next visit!"

STEPS TO REVISITING UNWANTED COMMANDS FOR TOUCH

Check-in: "What was it like?"

Validate: "That makes sense . . ."

Clarify Boundary: "It is not okay that . . ."

Reduce Embarrassment/Guilt/Shame: "I am so proud of you . . ."

Teach: "Next time . . ."

"Mary Grace, what was it like when Aunt Kathy told you to give her a hug?"

"I didn't like it," Mary Grace responded.

Next, Mom can validate Mary Grace's discomfort. "It makes so much sense that you didn't like it. I wouldn't have felt good hugging her either if I were you, since you just met her today. Even people I know for a little while, I don't always want to hug."

Then Mom clarifies the boundary. "It is not okay for anyone to expect you to let them touch you without you saying it is okay. Aunt Kathy made a mistake in asking for that. Do you have any questions about that?"

Assuming Mary Grace says no, her mom can reduce any embarrassment or guilt or shame she may feel by stating, "I am so proud of you for standing up for yourself and shaking your head. You were so brave. That's hard to do!"

Finally, she can close with a teachable moment: "Next time, you can do the same thing you did this time. You can shake your head and say no out loud. And if Mom/Dad are not around, you can also say just what I said to Aunt Kathy. Remember what I said?" If your kid doesn't remember, say it again. "I said, 'In my family, we can wave, smile, or hug when we say goodbye.' You can also say, 'I don't want to hug,' and wave."

MODELING "NO"

Children learn so much through modeling. Even innate skills, like eating and drinking, are not learned without modeling and support. So, too, it is with relating to the world around them. If we do not model how to say no effectively, who will?

This is where you can become a child's coach. We can't expect a child to learn after one time of discussing this, so, like before, be prepared to model this more than once. I want to share with you another story to illustrate this.

Alex is a six-year-old boy. His uncle, Jimmy, was visiting for the weekend. Alex's mom, Candace, is learning to coach Alex on how to say no. Uncle Jimmy and Alex were playing a game of checkers together. Alex was starting to get tired after a long day of activities and said, "I don't want to play anymore." Uncle Jimmy pouted and said, "You are making me sad. We need to finish this game." Candace stepped in. "Alex, you can stop playing if you want to. You have had lots of activities today. Are you ready for some rest time, or do you want to play something else? Before you change activities, make sure you help Uncle Jimmy clean up." She then turned to Uncle Jimmy and said, "Thanks so much for playing with Alex! We try to honor 'nos' whenever possible here, so as long as Alex helps you clean up, we can shift activities now."

Let's break down the important pieces of this. Uncle Jimmy, well-meaning as he may be, is conveying the message that Alex is not allowed to say no, because it "makes" Uncle Jimmy sad. This evokes guilt and sometimes shame in a child, and they get the message that their preferences are less important than pleasing another person, and in particular an adult. This is why Candace does the best thing when she intervenes directly to Alex first. Instead of focusing on redirecting Uncle Jimmy, whom she does not have responsibility for, she teaches Alex what he can do in the moment to respond. She gives him multiple options for what to do next, rather than forcing him to keep playing. She also indirectly communicates family rules to Uncle Jimmy, with the expectation that Uncle Jimmy will honor this in the future. Finally, she offers a warm expression of gratitude to him, rather than attacking or villainizing him for not knowing how to handle Alex's "no."

As we reflect more, we can see how Uncle Jimmy's comments, without intervention, can make Alex more susceptible to harmful messaging about boundaries. If Alex doesn't learn what his mom is teaching him, he may forget that he is allowed to say no. Instead, I want Alex to know that his comfort level matters, and that it is okay to make other people unhappy with him, if it involves setting a healthy boundary for himself.

I recognize that I am asking a lot of you as a caregiver in this. You could fear that your child will not be liked by the other adult. Many parents feel worried about being judged by others for their child's behavior. You can feel as if the child is an extension of your parenting ability (or lack thereof), which can also make it hard to encourage behavior that some adults will feel hurt by. You may also tend to be passive in your relationships with others in general, which makes breaking the pattern of staying silent really tough![2]

Whatever the things are that will make this difficult for you, take a moment to think of them now. Know that you are not alone in having these concerns and difficulties. It is so difficult to speak up. Pray for the courage, even now, to say something in these moments. It is the very best thing for your child and is a good opportunity for you to feel strong and empowered as well!

We *can* sometimes be harsh toward other parents when we feel scared or protective for our kids. This is why you can feel free to refrain from criticizing or villainizing the other adult. Some adults, perhaps like some reading, were never taught the importance of children having autonomy over their bodies. There is grace for these moments, as we all take steps to be more thoughtful and aware of how to protect children and honor their dignity.

At the same time, if a parent is offended by the boundary you set on behalf of your child, that is not your responsibility. Your responsibility is primarily to pay attention to the needs of your child and provide for them to the best of your ability. Also, if another parent or adult is not willing to hear a direct and calm boundary-setting, that is important to pay attention to. It may also determine how much time you are able to let your child be around them and whether they are allowed to watch your child when you aren't around.

MODELING OTHER BOUNDARIES

If we could guarantee that no one would hurt children, I would be much more inclined to say that there is no harm in encouraging your child to hug Uncle Trey and Aunt Keira. But that is not the world we live in. As we accept that reality, we can also take concrete steps, in this broken world of sin, to help keep our kids safe and thus help them move towards virtue with fewer barriers along the way.

It's no secret that many reports of childhood sexual abuse by clergy have surfaced in recent years. One striking thing about these reports is how certain clergy seemed to believe they were beyond reproach. They had a sense that their motives would not be questioned because of their role. This attitude is a red flag. It is important for you to know, and to teach to your children, that trust must be built, even with people in positions of authority.

No one is perfect, and as a result we must teach our children that even priests or pastors, friends, teachers, or family can prove themselves to be untrustworthy. Here's what this could look like in practice.

Let's imagine Fr. Andrew comes over for dinner. He is a new priest to your parish, is vibrant, fun, and seems great with kids! Because he is a younger priest, you hope he can be a good role model for your children. That is all well and good. So, how do you teach your children to begin building trust with Fr. Andrew?

Let's think proactively first. Before he (or any other adult or family) comes over, run over your ground rules for meeting new people: "Okay, kids, I wanted to say a few things before Fr. Andrew comes over for dinner tonight. We are eager to have him over, and we want to make him feel welcome. That means, when he comes in, you can say hello, wave, or smile to greet him. I will offer him a drink and invite him to sit down. All of these are ways to welcome him. Since you are just getting to know him, you may feel shy when he comes. That's because you are still getting to know him, and he is unfamiliar. You do not have to give him a hug hello or goodbye or sit on his lap either. Trust is built over time, and sometimes we don't want to touch people we don't know that well."

Now fast-forward. Fr. Andrew is at the house, and everything is going well. The kids have warmed up to him and want to give him a tour of the house. You can say something like this: "A tour is a great idea! No need to go upstairs, since all we do up there is sleep, but let's show all the common spaces, since that is where we hang out with our guests." This teaches your kids that there are spaces even in our homes that are private rather than common spaces, modeling boundaries. As the family builds trust with visitors, the children may want to show off their rooms. But for a first visit, this boundary is a good teachable moment. For future visits, a rule could be "Non-family only go in our bedrooms with a parent present."

One final thought before we wrap up this discussion. If someone expects you or your child to trust them intuitively because of their role, take note. This may mean, at best, that a person has a poor personal sense of boundaries. At worst, it can mean that a person would try to use their authority to manipulate. Setting up additional parameters and stronger boundaries with these people is critical for maintaining safety in your home.

You may be wondering, "What about times when I am not there to set limits for my child? How can I teach them to hold boundaries for themselves?" These are significant concerns, which is why we'll turn now to a discussion of how children learn to say no.

CHAPTER 5

"HOW DO THEY LEARN TO SAY NO?"

TEACHING BOUNDARIES FOR TIMES WHEN YOU AREN'T THERE

This chapter will coach you on how to model for children about saying no, setting limits, and honoring the limits and boundaries of others, specifically when you aren't around. This chapter will also lay out practical ways to speak to children about consent (without reducing the conversation to consent as the only gauge of what makes behavior acceptable or not).

PRACTICING HOW TO SAY NO

How do we teach a child that their no means no for times when we aren't around? Remember that practice is essential. You can prepare for the moments we talked about in the last chapter by setting aside a few minutes in a car ride or while doing another activity together to practice saying no.

If a kid is not willing to practice in a particular moment, you don't have to push it. We are building foundations for a series of talks, not just one. Try circling back at another time to role-play "no" moments. Here is how you can act out the scenario:

YOU: "Can we practice standing up for yourself when people try to get you to do something that is against our family rules?"
CHILD: "Sure."
YOU: "I will play you, and you can play the adult. Tell me to give you a hug."
CHILD: "Give me a hug!"
YOU: "In my house, we don't have to hug. We can wave or smile, too, when we say goodbye." [Wave goodbye and smile.]
CHILD: "But I really want a hug!"
YOU: "No, thank you. I don't want to. I wave goodbye usually. Bye." [Wave and smile.]

After you model the behavior, swap. Let your child play themselves, and you play the adult. If they are willing, try being an adult who pushes the child by trying to induce guilt or calling them "rude." Bonus points if you can make it a game and give a reward for it, reinforcing that these teachable moments can also be fun!

HONORING NO

Teaching children the power of their voice will foster trust and security as they experience a sense of autonomy over their bodies. Unless another person is stopping your child from doing something unsafe (such as running in the street,) it is important to respect your child's "no" to other people's physical touch and even celebrate it. This is true even when the behavior is inconvenient for you or others around you (like when you want them to sit on a friend's lap to free up a chair, and they refuse). Let's lay out some of the steps for modeling and honoring your child's "no" so that they can build confidence for moments when you aren't present.

1. Listen and watch for the "stop" or "no" moment.
2. Notice when another does not listen.
3. "Pause" the moment.
4. Clarify the "no."
5. Reinforce speaking up.
6. Redirect behavior in response to the boundary.

PARENTAL NUDITY

How old is too old for your child to see a parent naked? The answer is, it depends. What we know for sure is, when a child is not comfortable with parental nakedness, whether the parent notices it or not, such experiences can be harmful for a child. This is especially true when there is a sexualized connotation around the nudity, but not exclusively in that case. Some people will tell you that the gauge is the comfort of the child—that is, if the child and adult are both comfortable, it is okay. The hard part about this is that not every kid will tell a parent, especially when there isn't already open conversation about sexuality. Important cues are a child looking away or covering their body when changing, blushing or other signs of embarrassment when naked, and obviously if a child voices discomfort, listen.

On average, concepts like modesty and privacy start to make sense between ages four and eight, and children most often end up wanting privacy when naked by age seven to twelve.[1] In general, I would recommend that, when a child is around age four, you could start offering them the option to look away or leave the room when you change, and you could be more discreet with your changing when possible. As a child signals any verbal or nonverbal discomfort around your nakedness, make a point to acknowledge and validate their feelings: "That makes sense." Also, thank them for telling you: "I am so grateful you were honest and spoke up about that." Finally, tell them how you will change your behavior to honor their feelings: "In the future, I will make sure I cover up."

Let me give an example of what these steps can look like. I was recently playing with two five-year-old kids. One started tickling the other, who shrieked, "Stop!" The first kid did not stop. This is the moment for an adult to intervene.

I immediately said, "Pause. Let's stop playing for a minute." I turned to the kid who had shrieked, "Stop!" and said, "Do you want to be tickled?" She said, "No." I responded, "Good for you for noticing and speaking up about that!" That's the reinforcement piece. Celebrate the awareness your child has about their limit.

Then I turned to the other child and said, "She doesn't want to play that way. Can you come up with another way to play? Even when someone doesn't stop you, it's important to stop when someone says to."

This teaches a child to develop the flexibility and willingness to listen to someone and adjust their behaviors accordingly, rather than continuing to do the same thing. "Sure," this child said, and the two kids proceeded to pretend they were lions going on a journey.

There are also times when a child says no to playing a certain way, such as tickling or rough-and-tumble play, but then goes right back to tickling or tackling the other child. This also calls for a pause moment. Say something like this: "Remember when you said to stop? When we say, 'Stop,' it is important to listen to that. No means no. But if we go right back to what we said the other person should stop, it can be confusing for us and for them. When we say stop, we want to mean it and not go back to what we were doing before. Stop means stop, okay?" We want to enforce the idea that yes means yes and no means no. This can keep kids from sending mixed messages to themselves or to others in the future.

THE RELEVANCE OF TRUSTWORTHINESS

Relationships, and the level of closeness and intimacy within them, are supposed to convey the level of trust built between those people over time. It's worth teaching a child that trust depends on the trustworthiness of the adults a child is around. But how can we explain a word like "trustworthiness" to a child?

Have you ever made the mistake of trying to teach a concept to a child, only to realize they have no idea what the words you are using mean? This happened for me when trying to teach a little girl I nannied to "obey." She, like many of your children, seemed to take special delight in disobeying sometimes. This was especially true when it was time for bed. One night, she kept prancing out of her room as soon as she was placed in her bed. So, I thought it was time I should teach her to obey.

How did I do it? Well, I told her, "You need to obey. You need to listen. Show me how you obey by walking into your room and getting into bed." She repeated back, "Obey, obey, obey," and marched off to bed. As you can imagine, I was delighted and felt for sure we had made significant headway.

Only a few days later, we were spending some time at the neighborhood pool. I asked her to get out of the water to dry off. No sooner had she gotten out, she hopped right back in the water with a huge grin on her face. Me being the therapist-in-training I was, I figured I could showcase how well I had taught her to obey. I reminded her gently, "Show me how you obey." This time, she again sang out, "A-bey, a-bey, a-bey," but continued to swim. So, I asked her, "Do you know what O-bey means?" "Nope," she smiled, as she sang louder, "AH-BEY, AH-BEY, AH-BEY."

This story hopefully will help you to learn from my mistakes. We can use all kinds of words with kids, but if they do not know what the words mean, we are spinning our wheels.

Back to the drawing board. What does "trustworthiness" even mean? This is yet another one-minute talk to have.

"Honey, do you know what trustworthiness means / feels like? [Pause for answer.] To me, trustworthiness means that, when I am with someone, I feel safe, warm inside, secure, and like I can count on someone to do what they said they would do and not do what they said they wouldn't do. That's trustworthiness to me. How do you know someone is trustworthy?"

Helping a child define concepts like trustworthiness by sharing how it feels inside to trust someone is critical. Helping them identify what it feels like inside to trust someone, to feel safe, and to feel secure is how we help them build a sense of confidence in their own intuition. You can also share how you know you can trust someone who has shown themselves worthy of trust.

Here is a sample script for teaching trustworthiness:

> "I know I can really trust _____ because they (1) tell me the truth; (2) only ask me to do things that are good for me or help me grow; (3) do what they say they will do and are consistent; (4) care about what I think and respect my thoughts and feelings; (5) protect me from harm. Trust is earned, not owed."

Sometimes children assume the trustworthiness of adults too quickly. A critical lesson to teach a child is that people do not deserve your trust simply because they exist. Trust is built over time and experience. Just as you do not trust someone intuitively whom you see at a work conference or church event every six months, you ought not expect your child to trust someone they see a few times a year. Kids benefit from learning that some people are worthy of trusting and others are not, and that trust is built gradually for them as much as for all of us.

It can also be helpful to teach kids that there are degrees of trust that exist on a spectrum. This will be helpful for future relationships, romantic and otherwise, so laying the foundation in early childhood is ideal. What I mean by this is that I may trust someone with collecting my mail when I am out of town, but not trust that person with babysitting my child. I may trust someone with holding a newborn baby while I go to the bathroom, but not with bathing the baby without me present. I may trust someone I don't know well with doing my hair for a wedding, but not with being in a room while I change. Trust is impacted by many things but includes the role of the person in my life, their capacity to follow through, and the experiences I have had with that person up until this time. Illustrating this for a child may seem tricky, so let's see if some scripting can help.

> "There are people we can trust with everything and everyone we love, like God. God is perfectly trustworthy. Then there are people we can trust with most things. I trust Daddy to take care of you when I have to go somewhere, to love me no matter what, and to help the best he can. I trust Aunt Cara to babysit you when Daddy and I go out. I trust my neighbor to water the plants outside when we are out of town. I trust the cashier to give me the right change when I hand them money at the store. I trust different people differently, and you will too."

You can also make this conversational so that it is less of a lecture and more of a dialogue. You could ask your seven-year-old:

> "Who do you trust with everything? Who do you trust with feeding you and taking care of you? Who do you trust by giving them a kiss? Who do you trust by giving them a hug? Who do you trust with watching your pet? Who would you trust with your favorite toy for a day? See, we trust different people differently, and that's okay. And because trust is built, just because I trust someone (like my friend _______), that doesn't mean I expect you to. So, if you ever get a feeling in your belly that you don't trust someone, that is worth

> listening to. And you can always tell me when you feel that way. I will believe you and help you listen to that too."

What a valuable lesson when we teach a child to listen to the natural gut response they have to people. How many of us regret not paying attention to our gut, even as adults, after dismissing our reactions to a person as "judgmental" only to find out later that they end up confirming our fears. Sure, sometimes our gut response can be wrong, but there is a difference between *noticing* a gut response without acting on it and outright *dismissing* it. We want to do more noticing and less outright dismissing. I'll explain this a bit more to keep it from being so abstract.

Let's say you meet a mom at the park. You immediately have a gut sense of discomfort. You can't quite articulate why, but warning signs are going off.

Noticing it means you take stock of the situations and start to become curious as to what is happening. You may ask yourself, "Who does this person remind me of?" When you are at home later, you may call a friend and talk about it more to think about it more deeply. You may bring it up with a therapist or other guide. You may still be warm to the mom, and you may even be willing to talk to her again at the park, but you may do so with some level of distance until you can get to know her more.

Dismissing it means you tell yourself things like, "What is wrong with me? She seems fine!" You may make negative judgments about yourself for being "so critical." You may push past your discomfort by inviting her over for dinner, in the hopes that connecting more will help the feelings go away. You may say yes to every playdate, expecting things to get better with time. Eventually, your discomfort may subside, but more because you pushed past it than anything. Dismissing doesn't allow us to learn, which is one of the reasons it can be so harmful to growing a sense of intuition over time.

It will be important to teach your kids to notice rather than dismiss as well, especially when you aren't around. When they have a "gut feeling" about someone, you want to help them be curious about that. When it comes to noticing unhealthy or abusive behavior of others, we want to take cues from a child's behavior. To the best of your ability, be curious when your child is uninterested in spending time with someone or seems avoidant of certain people, places, or situations. Pay attention to changes in behavior and settings that trigger these. Be curious about why this might be, so you don't repeat the mistakes of other adults who have dismissed a child's avoidant behavior as defiance, when it was really a cry for help amid abuse.

STEREOTYPES THAT CAN COMPROMISE SAFETY

There are lots of stereotypes commonly held by parents that can put children at greater risk for unsafe environments and send the message that boundaries don't apply in certain contexts. These stereotypes are also well-known by perpetrators of child abuse, and they can exploit these stereotypes if we are not keeping our eyes open.

GENDER NORMS

I often hear from people that they feel more comfortable having their child around a woman than a man. There are a lot of valid reasons for this, since women more typically step into roles as babysitters or caregivers and are overrepresented in fields that involve caring for children. At the same time, this stereotype can lead parents to overlook signs of inappropriate behavior from women or to too quickly leave their child with a woman without vetting her.

For example, physical touch between women and children can be normalized too quickly, whereas a man at the same age befriending children, and particularly young girls, can raise red flags. This can lead to the normalization of contact that makes a child uncomfortable. It can mean assuming people are safe by virtue of their gender long before trust is built. This brings us to another assumption about sexual orientation that I want to highlight as well.

ASSUMPTIONS THAT ABUSE ONLY HAPPENS BETWEEN PEOPLE OF THE OPPOSITE SEX

I sometimes hear parents say things like, "I am so grateful I can trust our young boys with Fr. _____. It is so good to know they have a trustworthy male role model to take them on a retreat." Or "I am so grateful that my daughter goes to an all-girls' school. She doesn't have to worry about unwanted attention." After reading countless reports of how these exact scenarios can lead to the abuse of minors, I shudder at the sentiment.

These adults presume their children's safety because they assume that every adult only has the potential to abuse children of the opposite sex, and that people of the same sex are safer with one another than they are with the opposite sex.

This is simply not true in every case. Sexual abuse can also be perpetrated by older men against younger boys, or by older women against younger girls. The reality is that some people with pedophilia are attracted to children of both sexes, while some are exclusively attracted to one sex or the other.

It's also important to know that a sexual abuser's desire to sexually abuse a child isn't always related to that abuser's sexual orientation when it comes to sexual relationships with other adults. For example, an adult man might be primarily attracted to adult women and yet also enjoy the feeling of power that comes from sexually abusing a young person of either sex. This is one reason it's unhelpful to attribute the child abuse crisis in Catholic churches or in our communities at large as a "problem of homosexuality." Much of this abuse has indeed been perpetrated by adult men against boys—yet this may be, at least in part, because cultural assumptions about the safety of same-sex environments led to fewer boundaries in those environments. Adult men with a desire to abuse children of any sex, for any reason, most often had far more access to young boys (as in the cases of the Boy Scouts or Catholic priests with altar boys).

This caveat is important, because it is easy to scapegoat individuals who are attracted to the same sex as threats to children, while also presuming in our daily lives that same-sex environments are guaranteed secure spaces. Both of these assumptions do harm. The first assumption is unfair to sexual minorities, many of whom are not attracted to minors and are no more likely than anyone else to harm a child. The second assumption diminishes our ability to identify inappropriate behavior in same-sex contexts—especially if we feel confident that an adult is heterosexual based on their opposite-sex adult relationships and therefore assume they would never abuse a same-sex child.

TEACHING CONSENT

The concept of consent is an important one, even if it cannot be the sole gauge of healthy and whole adult sexual relationships. Simply put, consent means giving permission to another person. The idea of bodily consent assumes that each person is the gatekeeper of their own body. In Western culture, up until the last few decades, people rarely talked about vocalizing consent, making the assumption that if a person didn't say no, anything was fair game. This mindset has been shifting in recent years; physical touch, especially but not exclusively in the context of physical intimacy, now requires a clear "yes" rather than just a lack of "no."[2]

While not everything our culture teaches about consent today is necessarily good or helpful, the basic principle that people should have the power to deny someone else access to their body is true and valuable for children to understand. Understanding and practicing consent is an important skill in many relationships and is essential to the Sacrament of Marriage. Each person must come to marriage freely. Thus, teaching consent is one way to help prepare your children for marriage if that is their vocation. It is also a helpful and important piece of teaching children about their bodies and will give a good start when we come to book 2 of this series, where we will learn to teach teens about sexuality and move beyond consent-based approaches alone.

Just like the word "trust," "consent" won't mean anything to your child unless you help them understand it.

You could start by pointing out moments when they have a right to say yes or no:

> "When we say yes to playing a game or giving a hug, that's called giving consent, or permission. 'Consent' is a word that means saying yes to something we want. For instance, when I ask you if you want a bedtime story, and you say yes, you are consenting. You are giving me permission to read you a story. If you are jumping on the trampoline and your sister tackles you, and you say no, you are not giving consent—you are not giving permission. And that's why your sister needs to stop tackling you when you say no."

It is also valuable to differentiate times where a child's consent is not the ultimate decider of what happens next.

> "There are specific times when we will not honor your yes or no. These times involve moments when we need to do something to keep you safe. For example, if you run toward the road and I come to get you, I will pick you up even when you say no. That's because the street is where cars are, and if you run in the street, you can get hit. If you say you do not want to eat dinner, you still need to sit with the family. This is because eating is what gives your body energy to survive. It's the same with sleep. Even if you say you don't want to go to sleep, you still do need to because that helps your body grow strong and be healthy. Things like going to school and listening when a teacher says to be quiet, even when you don't want to, are other examples of when we expect you to listen even if you don't want to. But other than those things that we do for your good, if you say yes or no about your body, we and other people need to listen to it."

Now let's outline a few opportunities to teach your kids about setting and enforcing their own personal boundaries when you are not watching. These kinds of scenarios will arise more and more in social settings and in the home as your kids get older and more mobile. It's important to have "prep talks" with your kids before going into social settings, specifically with the goal of teaching about boundaries around touch.

Let's take the example of your whole family going to a birthday party. You could say, "Kids, we are going over to the house of a friend from church for a birthday party today. There will be lots of people there, some whom you know and some whom you don't. Let's remember the rules of being around other people."

PHYSICAL AFFECTION AT HELLO AND GOODBYE

"What are the ways we greet people and say goodbye? [We say hello/goodbye, and we can wave, smile, or even hug if we know the person well and want to.]"

PHYSICAL TOUCH

"If a person picks you up or hugs you or touches you some other way and you don't want that, you can say no. They should listen and stop. If they don't, come get me and I will help."

PLAY

"There will be activities for you to do [maybe a water-balloon fight, trampoline, sports, or rough-and-tumble play]. If you are playing and you want to stop a game, you can say clearly, 'I don't want to do this anymore.' The other person should listen and not make you keep playing. They may keep playing their game, but you can stop. If they don't allow you to stop, come get me and I will help."

PARENTAL PRESENCE

It's good to remind kids in social settings that trusted adults are around if they need help. Notice how this idea is subtly included in the last few examples: an acknowledgment that you, the parent, are around, and they can come find you if they need help. It doesn't hurt to make this reminder even more explicit as well:

> "Even though you will be playing with friends and having fun, if you are having a hard time or something is not good, you can always come find me. If you can't find me, ask someone to help you find me. Even if you can't see me, I am around and I want you to come let me know if you need something. That's true if you need to go to the bathroom or wash your hands and want help, if you're getting hungry and want some food, or if you're getting tired and want to rest a bit. Even if I am talking, you can come and put your hand on my shoulder to let me know you need something. Then, as soon as I finish what I'm in the middle of saying, I can help you."

Once you've established with your child how your family approaches personal boundaries, your next step as a parent is to lay out clear rules for your entire family and then to communicate those rules with others outside your family. That's what we'll address in the next chapter.

CHAPTER 6

"WHAT ARE GOOD HOUSE RULES, AND HOW DO I EXPLAIN OUR HOUSE RULES TO OTHER ADULTS?"

COMMUNICATING FAMILY BOUNDARIES TO NON-FAMILY MEMBERS

This chapter builds on the last chapter to help you identify concrete rules to guide your family, and then to figure out how to communicate those rules to people outside your home. You'll notice that this chapter and subsequent chapters are targeted more toward kids aged five to nine, when kids are more able to remember rules, share boundaries, and build verbal communication skills.

Some of the concrete rules we'll address are no secret keeping (an important rule that helps prevent potential abuse situations), no changing with other children, no group bath times, and other family rules that may be hard to enforce when a child is not at home.

Because you can't always enforce these rules when your child isn't with you, it's helpful to set boundaries with other adults as well. I want to begin by helping you identify the primary people you want to teach about your family rules. Then we'll discuss challenges to setting and maintaining boundaries with extended family members who may have different rules. Finally, I'll offer tips for starting these conversations with other adults in noncombative ways, while still asserting boundaries that protect your child.

SETTING FAMILY RULES

Before we think about communicating family rules to others, we first have to clearly identify these rules. This breakout box will give you some examples of possible family rules as a foundation.

EXAMPLES OF FAMILY RULES

- We do not keep secrets.
- We give others privacy when they are changing, going to the bathroom, or showering.
- We expect privacy when we are changing, going to the bathroom, or showering.
- We do not bathe with other people without our parent(s) present. We wear bathing suits in those cases.
- We can say no to physical touch, even with family members.
- We can greet and leave people with a wave, hug, smile, or verbal hello or goodbye.
- Our private parts are good and worth protecting. They belong to us. No one can touch them without our permission and without our parent present, no matter what.
- We do not touch other peoples' private areas or our own private areas when we're with other people.
- We do not let other people touch our private areas unless a parent is supervising us at the doctor's office.
- A parent's job is to help protect us. If someone makes us feel uncomfortable, scared, angry, or embarrassed, we help our parents do their job by telling them about it.
- We do not go in a friend's bedroom without our parent's permission, and we do not play with friends in our bedroom without our parent's permission. Bedrooms are for sleeping. We can play in

rooms that are open. If our bedroom is a play space, we keep the door open and tell a parent before we go there.

- We leave doors open and unlocked when we are playing with friends. This helps us get help if we ever need it.

NO SECRET KEEPING

A foundational rule to teach kids is that there is no secret keeping in a family. There can be specific exceptions to this rule (for example, some families might decide not to tell what they got each other for Christmas), but the rule as a whole is critical for several reasons. Many perpetrators of abuse will tell a child not to tell their parents; they might even say that if the child does tell, they will get in trouble. Some abusers will start by grooming a child—buying them secret gifts or offering to do so in the future and telling them not to tell anyone. Some will even go as far to say, "Your parents will give you away if you tell them what I did." This is a horrible reality, and we should do our best to protect our children from this.

To be proactive against this type of messaging, you can explain to a child, "We don't keep secrets in our family, but we do love surprises!" You can also say, "If someone ever tells you that you will get in more trouble for telling us the truth, remember this: You will *never* get in more trouble for being honest. And if someone tells you to keep a secret from us, and you do keep the secret for a little while but then tell us later, you will not get in trouble when you tell us. We will be proud of you that you told us when you did, even if some time has gone by."

Even if a secret is not in the context of abuse, for a child to keep secrets from their parents is not necessary or healthy. Secrecy reinforces shame: the feeling that "if you knew this part of me, you would reject me. So instead, I will hold you at arm's length, and I will reject myself in the isolation." Shame breeds dysfunction in our lives. This is one of the reasons why teaching a child that the truth is always better will help build communication and trust over time.

If a child can tell that you are feeling too fragile to receive the truth, they will lie in hopes that it is helping. We never want a child to be in the position of trying to take care of our emotions as adults. This is why we want to send the message that the truth, no matter how difficult it might be to receive, is always better than secrets.

DEVELOPING FAMILY RULES

- Set up a time to discuss family rules with your spouse.
- Get feedback from trusted adults and/or a therapist about possible rules.
- Agree on these with your spouse, and write out the rules.
- Schedule a family conversation; share these rules with kids, and give examples of what to do when rules get broken.
- Once a year, reiterate your rules and see about adding others, since these rules can evolve as children get older.
- As kids get older, they can be part of these conversations to help them feel involved in shaping their family culture.

If you are a caregiver of children who are not in your family, you can also take time to think through what rules and expectations you want to communicate to those in your care, especially if their families don't abide by some of the principles listed above.

WHOM TO TALK TO ABOUT FAMILY RULES

After developing family rules, it's important to think through whom we talk to about family rules. Who outside of your family needs to know about these rules so that they can abide by them, reinforce them, and intervene in moments when the rules are being broken? I recommend sharing these rules with anyone who will have one-on-one contact with your child, especially those who will have one-on-one contact when you are not around.

This includes teachers, daycare staff, babysitters / nannies, grandparents, any other extended family members who regularly care for your child, and close family friends.

An easy way to communicate your family rules is to make a 4x6 card and write them out. This card could also include other guidance for caregivers, such as any dietary restrictions, allergies, or special tips. If you are feeling extra creative, you could laminate the card and make copies for several people to have at once. This becomes especially important if you have children in a setting where multiple people will be in charge of their care (as can be the case with babysitters or daycare staff who rotate shifts).

This approach might feel over-the-top to some readers. You might feel as if you are making a mountain out of a molehill. But I want to encourage you that any steps you take to establish consistency and protect your child from future abuse are worth it. I am not encouraging helicopter parenting. In fact, having times when you are not with your child builds trust, is a way of recognizing your child's growing autonomy, and is healthy for parents and other caregivers. So when you are proactive about communicating your family's rules to other caregivers, don't think of this as helicopter parenting or paranoia. Instead, think of it as a way to ensure that you can safely leave your child with trusted others and *not* allow paranoia to drive your parenting. Preparation and planning equip you and your kids for daily life, rather than shielding them from it.

BABYSITTERS AND NANNIES

A babysitter is given significant authority over a child. This is no small thing, even if just for a few hours. Sadly, babysitters and nannies do sometimes perpetrate abuse against children. This is why it's risky to allow someone you and your kids don't already know and trust to babysit. Too often, when we're in a bind, we will entrust our children to people they have never met. Even one-time babysitters can do harm, perhaps more so if they know they are unlikely to ever see your family again. I think of a dear friend, Cullen, who was molested as a six-year-old by an extended family member who only babysat one time. I say this not to induce paranoia in you, but to reckon with the reality of childhood sexual abuse and highlight our responsibility in working diligently to reduce its likelihood.

Regular sitters are better than one-time arrangements. This allows you to build trust over time and establish consistency with caretakers. I recognize this is not always possible, but in the grand scheme of things it is best to reschedule or cancel an event if it means being able to abide by your family rules.

Imagine that you have plans to go to a birthday dinner for a friend. Your typical babysitter gets sick with the flu and can no longer watch your two children. Her mom reaches out to you to let you know the morning of the birthday dinner. She says that she is really sorry and reached out to a neighbor of hers who has a similarly aged daughter. She says, "I am happy to give you their number, since the neighbor said her daughter is free to help in my daughter's place!"

What do you do next?

I would recommend you not go to the dinner when you won't possibly be able to vet a new babysitter so quickly. This is disappointing, to be sure. It can also feel tricky to turn down a parent who went the extra mile to try to find an alternative. Assuming you plan to turn down the offer, here is a polite way to do so:

> "Thank you so much for letting me know and trying to find an alternative option. We will reach out to a backup babysitter we have and see if she is available. If not, we will plan to stay home this time, but we appreciate the extra effort you put into giving us other another possibility. I hope your daughter feels better!"

You could always give more insight into why if asked, saying something like, "In our family, we only allow babysitters our kids have gotten to know." But this isn't necessary. Too often, we feel as if we owe people an explanation for the boundaries we decide to set. The truth is, people do not have to understand or agree with our boundaries in order to respect them.

If you are hiring a babysitter or nanny, try to schedule one or more times when the sitter comes and watches your children with at least one parent or another trusted adult present to observe. Watch the interactions between the babysitter and your child. After this observation, if possible, schedule a time when the sitter is watching your children while you are home. Come into the room spontaneously to see how the sitter treats your child when they think you are not watching. We test-drive cars and sample food before buying. How much more important is it to "test" those who are caring for our children?

Sometimes, in the reality of daily life, you will get into a pinch and someone will watch your child before you have built trust. If so, we can plan for following up with your child after the fact. This will allow you to monitor whether the babysitter was a good fit and if anything concerning happened while you were gone. Even with regular sitters, you will want to check in with your child regularly to ensure that nothing is happening that compromises your child's safety. A trusted babysitter does not always translate to a safe babysitter.

Debriefing moments when you are not around is so helpful in continuing to cultivate open communication with your child for years to come.

DEBRIEFING A BABYSITTER EXPERIENCE

Here are several questions to ask after a child is left with a babysitter, especially if the babysitter is new, but not only then. Remember, most children are abused by someone the parents already know and believe they can trust.

- Ask general questions: "How was your time with _____? What did you think of _____? What did you do together?"
- Check in on rule implementation: "Sometimes [new] babysitters don't follow all the rules. How did _____ do with following our family rules?"
- Ask about inappropriate touch specifically: "Were there any moments when _____ touched you in a way you didn't like? How about moments when they touched your penis [or vulva]? Okay, just checking, since that's a really important family rule."
- Ask about comfort specifically: "Mom and Dad always want to make sure you are comfortable with the people we leave you with when we aren't home. Did you feel comfortable with _____? If not, what happened that made you uncomfortable? Would you

want _____ to babysit again, or would you like us to find someone else next time?"

NAVIGATING DIFFERING RULES

Not every family has the same rules. Maybe in your family it is known that children only get bathed by their parents. But maybe when your child is staying with their cousins, they have different rules. Take Carl, for example. Carl is a single dad, and he travels sometimes for work. He often reaches out to his sister, a mom of three, to watch his little boy, Andy, who is five. Carl has made it clear to Andy that only Dad can bathe Andy, unless Dad tells him otherwise, and that Andy is not to get into a bath with other people.

While Carl is out of town, he gets a call from his sister right before Andy's bedtime. When Carl asks how things are going, she says that Andy "was acting bad at bath time but seems better now." When Carl asks about what happened, his sister explains that her oldest child, Andy's twelve-year-old cousin, was helping with bedtime and went to give his two younger siblings and Andy a bath. "Andy freaked out," she says. "He kept saying, 'No!' and we didn't get why. We told him he had to take a bath or he couldn't get a bedtime story. He finally listened. You would've thought we were asking him to do something terrible."

Ideally, Carl would have told his sister ahead of time about their family rules, including bath time rules. He could also have talked with Andy about how it would be okay to take a bath supervised by his aunt. But let's assume that Carl is not actually comfortable with Andy being bathed together with all his cousins, supervised by an older cousin. This would be a fine rule to have, but it can feel risky for him to share this with his sister. After all, he already feels guilty for all the times he asks her to watch Andy. What if she feels hurt and defensive and doesn't want to help anymore?

Carl has a decision to make. Will he stand up for his child and take the risk of his sister not understanding his rule or feeling offended when he sets the boundary? Or will he act as if everything is fine?

I would encourage Carl to take a step of courage here, risky as it may seem. He can start by saying, "Oh, I know why Andy was saying no and acting that way. He was trying to follow our family rules, but I didn't tell him you all have different rules. I could have told you sooner about our family rules for bath time, so I am sorry for not prepping you. I don't let Andy take a bath with other kids, even family. It's just our family rules. Again, I understand you couldn't have known, but in the future, I would ask that you be the one to bathe him and, if you are going to do it with the cousins, that they wear bathing suits for it."

Carl's sister could respond in a couple of different ways. Maybe she is understanding and accepting of this boundary. It would be understandable if she was to go back to Andy and apologize for asking him to do something outside of his family rules. It would be better still if she explained the miscommunication. It is trickier if she becomes defensive. Let's imagine that happens.

Carl's sister, becoming upset, says, "Are you kidding me? Are you saying you think my son would do something to hurt Andy? He would never. And why would I need to have them wear bathing suits? My kids always bathe together, and it is no big deal. Why are you making a big deal out of nothing? It's just a bath."

If Carl is feeling defensive and protective of Andy, that would be understandable. Yet it's helpful to have these talks with other adults when things are calm. Maybe Carl has had a long day. If he is having trouble staying calm, he may say to his sister, "Listen, this conversation is really important to me. I know you are upset by me saying this, and I am grateful you are watching Andy. I also know I am wiped out from the day. Can we talk about this tomorrow when we have rested on it?"

If this is the approach Carl takes, it's important for him to circle back later. This is one of the biggest challenges we face when it comes to assertive conversations. Avoidance is so desirable, because it means delaying what is uncomfortable. And to be sure, having a conversation like this with a sibling—or anyone, for that matter—is not easy.

TIPS FOR HARD CONVERSATIONS

How do you more effectively have hard conversations with adults who have different boundaries than you, or those who unknowingly did not honor your family rules? If you are like most people, these conversations feel less impossible if you have concrete examples of how to approach the conversation and what to say. That's why this chapter is full of these examples.

As we saw in Carl's situation, one of the first things to consider is whether you and the adult you're talking with are calm enough to have a conversation like this one. Whenever possible, it's best to talk about serious and complex topics (such as boundaries) when you are calm and can set aside the time and energy for it. This sets you up for greater success. When we are feeling defensive, we struggle to problem-solve, tend to think in a more black-and-white way, and struggle to see through the eyes of the other person. This does us no favors in these conversations. If necessary, don't be afraid to press "pause" on your conversation, taking a break when someone becomes defensive.

Next, try scheduling the conversation ahead of time. This will allow you to have accountability around the conversation. I often invite a client to text or write an email during our session to set up a conversation with someone, especially if it is a hard conversation they have been avoiding. This makes it much more likely that they will end up having the conversation. Schedule the conversation for a time when you are likely to have the time and space to talk.

Write down what you want to say ahead of time, to keep it clear. Briefly name the topic(s) you want to address in the conversation and a summary of the main points. You could certainly bring your written notes to the conversation to keep your ideas clear, especially if the conversation is happening over the phone.

When you begin talking with the other adult, it might be helpful to acknowledge the difficulty of having this conversation *and* the importance of doing so. This allows for a bit of vulnerability right from the start, and it can take us out of a defensive posture toward someone else.

Recognize that different perspectives on these topics are common, and you do not need to villainize the other person simply because they hold a different perspective or take a different approach with their own kids. Here's the kind of thing you might want to say in this conversation:

> "Thanks so much for being willing to talk. I wanted to talk about what happened the other day with [bath time]. It is a difficult thing for me to bring up, and it is also really important to me that we can find common ground on this, since it involves our kids. I know that different people think differently about [this circumstance: bath time, physical touch, etc.]. We may have different approaches, and that's okay.
>
> What I would ask from you is that you respect my approach to parenting just as I want to respect yours. That means that, even when we have different rules, I will adjust to implementing your rules when I am around your children, and I would ask for the same when you are around mine.
>
> This is important to me because it offers consistency to my child and is a good lesson for them to learn. I'd love for you to be one of the trustworthy people in my child's life who helps reinforce this lesson for them."

The person you're talking with could respond in a variety of ways. Some adults will respond with curiosity, questions, and willingness to reinforce your boundaries. Others will shut down, become aggressive, or critique you.

It is obviously easier if the other adult responds by saying something like, "Even though we have different approaches, I will definitely follow these guidelines with your kid in the future and explain your family's rules to my kids as well. You are right—it's a good opportunity to remember we can do things differently as parents and still support one another. We don't want to undermine each other's authority."

But what if a parent or other adult doesn't respond well? What if their responses are critical and don't communicate willingness to make these adjustments? This will mean setting a firmer boundary in the future.

SETTING FIRMER BOUNDARIES WHEN NEEDED

Here's a way you could respond to an adult who isn't willing to follow your family's boundaries when they are with your child:

> "It sounds like you are not willing to respect this boundary because you do it differently. Unfortunately, that means I won't be able to allow ______ to happen again until we can

> come to an agreement. In the meantime, that will mean I won't be asking you to watch ______ when I'm not around. I'd still love for our families to spend time together, but I'd need to be around to supervise so that I can continue enforcing my family's rules consistently."

In having direct conversations with other adults, we are practicing assertiveness, which is communicating directly and honestly with others. The key is to "say what you mean, but don't say it mean." If you're struggling to do this well, review the pointers you've learned in this chapter, seek out support from others, and ask God for help in prayer.

It's much more difficult to communicate thoughtfully and clearly when emotions are running. In the next chapter, we will think through how to respond to your child in moments when your emotions are heightened because something has gone wrong.

CHAPTER 7

"WHAT DO I DO IF THEY TELL ME SOMETHING BAD HAPPENED TO THEM?"

RESPONDING TO UNWANTED SEXUAL EXPERIENCES

This book is meant to help you be a trustworthy person for the child or children entrusted to you. Your role is essential in establishing and maintaining their safety. It is no easy task, but there are few things more important than protecting an innocent child from harm. Despite your best efforts, however, there may be times when someone harms a child in your care. In a world where evil occurs, I want to equip you to know how to respond in even the darkest of moments.

Whether you are a parent, educator, caregiver, or trusted adult, I hope you never have to use the skills I will teach you in this chapter. But it's important that you know how to respond when a child has been harmed. The more you know, the more quickly you can get a child the support they need. This chapter will offer guidance, but please know that it is not a replacement for the support of a competent therapist.

TRIGGER WARNING

Trigger warning: I want to recognize with real tenderness that many of you reading have experienced your own painful childhood abuse. Maybe you haven't yet processed those experiences fully. Or maybe you've spent years diligently working to heal. Either way, reading a chapter about childhood abuse will likely stir up painful emotions. Please take care of yourself as you move through this chapter. I don't say this because you're fragile—you are not fragile. But the reality is, stories that mirror our own hit us differently. Be gentle with yourself as you read, and take breaks or come back later if you find that it is not the right time to read this chapter.

Consider this example. Jay was an eight-year-old boy who often spent time at his cousins' house across the street. He had two older cousins, both boys as well; one was ten and one was thirteen. Jay always looked up to his cousins and would often beg to spend time with them and go over for sleepovers. It seemed out of the blue when Jay started to say he didn't like his cousins anymore and didn't want to spend time with them. At first, Jay's parents continued to encourage him to spend time with his cousins and redirected him when he said, "I hate them." After a while, Jay's dad started to wonder if there was a reason for this change. He thought, "Maybe they are teasing him, or they don't have the same interests anymore because they are older than Jay." One day, he brought it up to Jay, asking, "Jay, you have said you hate your cousins. Can you tell me why?"

Jay seemed to shut down when his dad asked this and said he didn't want to talk about it. Jay's dad stayed calm and replied, "I see that this is not something you want to talk about right now. Remember, we don't keep secrets in our family, and I can understand if it's hard to talk about. No one can force you to talk about it, and I would never force you to talk about it, but I want to make sure we can talk about these things. I love you, and nothing you tell me will make me love you less. Nothing."

Jay didn't respond, but his dad's approach helped him. Since Dad wasn't forcing him to tell more, he started to feel more willing to actually say something. When his dad expressed his unconditional love, Jay felt a bit more assured. He also picked up on how calm Dad seemed, which made him feel that Dad could handle what he had to share.

Even though Jay didn't respond, Dad continued, "Until we can understand more of what is going on, you do not have to spend time with your cousins without Mom or Dad around. Would that help?" Jay nodded yes and left it at that.

A few weeks later, when Dad was talking with Jay about his day and praying with him before bed, Jay started to cry. Dad calmly hugged Jay before asking a question: "Do you know what is making you cry?" Jay nodded, still crying. Dad reassured Jay again calmly, even though he was starting to feel more worried. "You can tell me. What's up?" It was then that Jay started to share. Over the course of the past year, his older cousin and younger cousin began to show him their penises. Gradually, the older cousin began to give the younger cousin oral sex, and then requested the same from the younger cousin. Jay had been forced to watch. This is when Jay started to say he didn't want to spend time with them.

How is a parent to respond when this happens?

RESPONDING TO DISCLOSURE

First, say this: "Thank you so much for being so brave and telling me. I imagine that was really hard to say, and I am so grateful you told me."

Next, calmly and clearly say this: "I believe you. What your cousins did to you was not okay. And it was not your fault."

Third, validate: "It makes so much sense that you didn't want to spend time with them. I shouldn't have put any pressure on you to see them, and now I understand. I am sorry I did that. I am so impressed you noticed that you didn't want to, that you listened to that feeling, and that you told me."

Fourth, tell the child about their fundamental goodness which is not changed by this: "I am so proud of you and the person you are. What happened with your cousins doesn't change your value one bit. You are good and precious."

Fifth, offer assurance, saying only what you can follow through on: "I will help you make a plan for what to do from here. For now, is it okay if we invite Jesus into this moment? We are never alone, especially when we are in pain and feel alone. He knows your pain and loves you so much. He will help us find a way forward."

In the coming days, weeks, and months, continue to reiterate how much you love your child, how precious and good they are, and that this was not their fault in any way. One of the most common core beliefs that stems from traumatic experiences is, "I am bad." Your presence, as an adult who is trusted, has more power than you know in telling a child, "You are not bad. You are so precious and good. This was not your fault. Nothing will ever change how lovable you are. I will help you through this. You are not alone."

WHAT IF THEY ASK ME NOT TO TELL ANYONE?

Never promise a child that you will not tell others what they are about to say to you. If a child asks this, say something like this back: "Your safety is so important to me. I will do whatever it takes to make sure you are safe to the degree I can. Since I can't know what you are going to say, I can't promise that I won't tell anyone. If I need to tell someone to help keep you protected, I will do that. I will not tell anyone without you knowing who I am telling, and if you want, you can be there while I talk with them."

SEEK OUTSIDE HELP

You are not supposed to know how to handle these moments. Any time a child is harmed, the world is not how it is supposed to be. Abuse is tragic each and every time. Don't expect yourself to have all the answers or know the right things to say and do without support. Call for help as soon as possible.

Asking for help might involve calling a trusted friend to have a sounding board. It will also certainly involve contacting a mental-health or medical professional to determine next steps. A trained professional is the best person to help you determine when and how to involve local law enforcement and Child Protective Services (CPS), with the actual name of this agency varying state by state. Your young child does not need to be part of these initial calls. You can protect them from the overwhelming nature of this system by taking the reins and getting them the support they need, while buffering them against the system.

AVOID DETECTIVE MODE

While you always want to make space for your child to share as much as they want to share, resist the urge to move into detective mode. This will likely be very uncomfortable for you. Those detailed questions can come later. Before you ask more detailed questions, it is important to say, "It's okay if you don't remember it all." That reduces the pressure a child can feel to "get it right," in an already difficult conversation. Later, you can ask, "What else do you remember about what happened?" "How many times?" If you are noticing that you are asking a lot of questions, perhaps out of your own sense of urgency, and your child seems overwhelmed, disconnected, or scared, slow down. Pause the questioning, which can make your child feel even more overwhelmed and less likely to open up. Say something like, "This is a lot to talk about, isn't it? I can see you are shutting down, which is our brain's way of saying we are done talking about this right now. Can we talk about this later?"

FIND WAYS TO GIVE CHOICES

One of the most impactful consequences of childhood sexual abuse, and all experiences of trauma, is that they exceed our capacity to cope. This leads a person to feel powerless in the aftermath of abuse. It is so important to give an abuse survivor choices, whenever possible, to help them know that they can begin taking their power back, even in seemingly small ways.

A trusted therapist can help you think through exactly what this looks like, but here are a few examples of ways to give choices:

"Honey, do you want me to stay with you as you fall asleep, or do you want some space as you sleep?"

"For breakfast, I made pancakes and bacon and eggs. What would you like?"

Some of these choices you offer your child will directly relate to what happened. For many parents, it can feel strange to invite children into the process of responding to a situation like this one. But this is yet another way of offering choices to your child, albeit the kind of choices we never want a child to have to face.

For example, you can ask a child whether they'd like to be present when you talk with authorities about what happened. Older children and teens might choose to be involved in the process of filing a report. And children of any age who have survived a trauma can evaluate their need to rest and recover: "Do you want to go to school tomorrow, or do you want to stay home?"

Again, I know these feel like daunting choices to give to a child. They are. And yet we know that returning autonomy to the person who has experienced trauma is key to reestablishing their sense of agency. With my clients, I call this "taking your power back." The sooner we can help someone know that they can take their power back and learn to cope with the unimaginable, the better.

COMMON FEELINGS AND THOUGHTS IN RESPONSE TO ABUSE

- Anger: "Why didn't I stop it?"
- Despair: "What's the point now?"
- Shock: "Did that really happen?"
- Fear of getting in trouble: "Are you mad at me?"
- Excessive Guilt: "I did something wrong."
- Shame: "I am bad."
- Excessive responsibility for occurrence(s): "I wanted it. It was my fault."
- Embarrassment: "Don't look at me. I don't want anyone to know."
- Numbness/Emptiness: "I don't feel anything."
- Sadness: "Why did this happen to me?"
- Panic: "Oh, no. Is it going to happen again? Will people find out? What will they think?"
- Disgust: "I feel gross."
- Protectiveness of perpetrator: "They didn't mean to. Don't be mad at them."

- Denial: "Nothing happened."
- Minimization: "It wasn't that bad. It wasn't a big deal. I just felt a little weird."

VALIDATING CONFLICTED EMOTIONS

Children who have survived abuse carry many emotions, including shame, embarrassment, blame, disgust, and fear.[1] They may also feel protective of the perpetrator of their abuse. This can be hard to understand until we recognize that some perpetrators have worked hard to establish a strong connection with a child. These conflicted emotions make it incredibly difficult for a child—or anyone—to make sense of their experience.

As a trusted adult, you can help with this. Begin by validating the emotions a child is feeling. Many parents fear that, by validating their child's emotion, they are saying that they agree with the emotion. They might worry that they will increase the intensity of their child's emotion and make things worse.

In practice, though, we find that when we validate another person's emotions through simple phrases like "Sure," "That makes so much sense," and "I hear you," this actually helps them process their emotions in a healthy way. When we validate a child's emotions, we aren't making a judgment about particular thoughts or perspectives; rather, we're recognizing the validity of the emotional experience they are having.

What is validation, anyway? At its core, validation is seeing the other person, acknowledging their internal experience, and accepting it as valid. It's saying, "It makes sense that you are thinking / feeling that way, and I see you where you are."

A key part of validation is mirroring. This means "holding up a mirror" to the other person and reflecting back to them what we see and hear. This technique is best done tentatively, both in our tone and in our actual phrasing, to leave room for correction. When I mirror what a person has said, I usually repeat back what I am hearing in different words, and then ask, "What would you tweak or say differently?" This gives a child or adult the freedom to correct me, and I welcome that correction.

Other important pieces of validation are making eye contact, eliminating distractions (for example, putting phones away and turning televisions off), leaning into the child to show interest and readiness to receive, and nodding periodically to show you are following what they are saying.

How do we use validation when responding to sexual abuse in a child? We mirror back what we perceive is happening in the child emotionally and say, "Oh, that makes sense that you are feeling ____."

VALIDATING STATEMENTS

- "It makes sense that you are feeling _____, especially given _____."
- "Did I get that right? What am I missing?"
- "Of course, that makes so much sense to me."
- "I hear you."
- "That is such an understandable feeling, because _____."

Sometimes, the best form of validation is showing our authentic emotional response to someone. This is a hard balance to strike when we're talking to a child. We don't want the child to believe they are hurting us or causing us pain, or that they need to take care of our emotional experience. At the same time, survivors of child sexual abuse often share how much it meant to them to have an adult show emotion on their behalf (for example, anger at the injustice, or sadness and tearfulness on their behalf). So don't be afraid to connect to those feelings when you are with a child. It's okay to say, "I am angry because they hurt you and that was wrong."

Being specific will help protect your child from believing they are responsible for the emotions you feel. You can even be clear and say, "I am tearing up because I feel sad and angry that this happened to you. It was not okay. I am so grateful you told me what happened. It is not your job to take care of me. I have the support of adults, and I will be okay. I am going to help us find a way forward."

ANSWERING THE TOUGH QUESTIONS

It is normal for your child to have tough questions about what happened. This is why finding a trauma-informed child therapist is a key early intervention. The longer you wait, the easier it is for life to seemingly go back to normal, even though internally your child will struggle to return to normalcy. In a real sense, they can't go back to the life they knew before.

Common questions (whether or not they are spoken aloud) from children who have been sexually abused include the following:

- Why did this happen to me?
- Who can I talk to about this?
- What do I do when memories come up?
- What does it mean if I felt some pleasure when it happened?

It's important to give a child trusting places to bring their questions. While talking with you and other caregivers has value, therapy is also crucial. Elementary-school children who quickly see a competent child therapist—especially one who works with survivors of trauma—can heal in significant ways from their abuse by their early teen years.

If you don't know the answer to a difficult question your child asks, it's okay to say so. Believe it or not, sometimes admitting your uncertainty actually helps.

Let me give an example of what I mean. Imagine a child asks you, "Why did this happen to me? What did I do wrong?" You can respond by first mirroring what you hear:

> "I hear you asking such hard and important questions, like 'How did this happen?' I also hear you wanting to know what you did to cause this. If I were in your shoes, I would ask that too. It makes sense that you are trying to figure out 'why.' And I don't know why this happened to you. I feel angry and sad that it happened, because what happened to you was not okay. But even though I don't know why it happened, I do know that it wasn't your fault. You did not cause this, and you did nothing wrong."

This type of response acknowledges both what you don't know—why this happened—and what you do know—that the child is not to blame. This is critical, and it's something you can say over and over again. This repetition will challenge the deep shame and guilt that a child can carry after sexual abuse. It is no small thing to challenge this shame and guilt as often as possible.

The question of pleasure is another common, but more often unspoken, one. A child will likely feel shame and embarrassment about their body's physical response to abuse. They may not even say something as clear as "Why did I feel pleasure?" They're more likely to say, "I think I wanted it." In fact, many kids will never acknowledge this feeling, even much later in life.

Why do children often feel arousal in response to sexual trauma? It's because the body generally responds to stimulation, even when that stimulation is unwanted. Even unwanted sexual touch can still cause a body to respond in ways that involve pleasure. This can be incredibly confusing for a child or adult who experiences sexual abuse. It is crucial to say to a child, "Feeling pleasure is a *normal* response. Anyone would feel pleasure if they were being touched in that way." Make this clear as well: "Feeling pleasure is different from agreeing to a behavior or having the ability to say yes to it. Just because you felt pleasure, that does *not* mean you wanted it or chose it. It's not your fault."

Perpetrators of sexual violence understand this confusion and will work hard to induce sensory stimulation and subsequent pleasure, using this as another weapon to keep a child quiet. Some will say, "See, you want this, you like this," making it more likely that a child will remain in a state of shame and silence. You can protect your child by challenging this messaging head-on. We have an important job as adults to speak truth into these moments when lies can so easily get in and complicate the healing process.

TAKING STEPS TO REESTABLISH SAFETY

I talked earlier about the importance of giving children choices in the aftermath of a disclosure of abuse. It's also important to find other ways to reestablish safety. This is no easy task and will require creativity and diligence along the way.

Routines can help a child restore their sense of consistency in life, which can help with reestablishing safety. Some children may actually want to return to school fairly quickly because of their longing for normalcy. After consulting with a therapist who knows your child, you can discern what timing will be best.

Because some kids will have intrusive memories of the incident(s), it is important to ask a child about these memories. With a young child, you could ask something like, "Do you ever have pictures of what happened with _____ in your mind?" Intrusive memories can lead to a strong sense of violation and lack of safety. When we can't seem to stop thoughts and memories from appearing in our minds, we might feel just as powerless and overwhelmed as we did when the original event(s) occurred. This feeling can be especially hard for a young child, who may not have the language to tell you when a memory is coming to mind.

It can be helpful for a child to come up with a code word, a symbol, or a visible sign that they can use to "show" when something painful is coming up in their minds. This way, they can learn to communicate in moments of pain even when they can't verbally tell you that something is wrong. For example, a child could take a trusted adult's hand and squeeze it twice, pass the adult a small note with a code word written down, or decide on another sign that is easy to manage in a moment of pain. This will help the child know that they can communicate what is happening, even without words. If this happens in a public space, taking the child to a private, quiet space can help them regain grounding.

One additional important way to reestablish safety is to allow your child to rediscover their voice. Refrain from speaking *for* them or *over* them, even when it feels difficult to be patient as they sort through their experience and learn to put language to it. Listen closely and find ways to elevate their voice when possible. Talia put it beautifully when she reflected on what she wished her parents had done in the aftermath of her childhood trauma:

> "Let me use my voice. One's ability to articulate does not develop in a vacuum. The only way I can feel more confident in using my voice to speak for myself, for others, etc. is by practicing this skill with people I have built trust with and I know love me. Let me stumble. Let me clarify. Let me contradict. Let me muddle my way through. Let me give voice to my internal experience. Please listen to me. Please

believe me. Please seek to understand me. Please help me learn to understand that what I am feeling won't kill me."

Here are some of the many concrete skills that can help a child reestablish safety and survive feelings that overwhelm them. These can be divided into internal safety skills (skills that help a child feel safe in their body again) and environmental safety skills (skills that help them feel safe in their environment). While approaches like these can work with people of any age, all of them are simple enough for a child to understand and put into practice.

INTERNAL SAFETY SKILLS

- *5-4-3-2-1 Grounding*: Name and describe 5 things you see, 4 things you touch, 3 things you can hear, 2 things you can taste, and 1 thing you can smell. This is a great distractor that allows you to access your body and your surroundings safely. You can do this with a child, each taking turns saying out loud what you see. If the child can't talk because they are overwhelmed, you can model the activity for them first.
- *Deep Breathing*: There are all kinds of great ways to practice deep breathing to establish a sense of power and control over your body. A therapist can help a child find the strategies that work best.

SQUARE BREATHING

One deep-breathing skill that I like to guide kids in is called square breathing or box breathing. It is accessible for children because it helps them visualize something they know—a shape. It can help a child go to sleep or simply calm their body. The child begins breathing in as they trace or imaginatively trace the edge of one side of a box. They then breathe out as they trace or imaginatively trace the edge of the next side. They repeat this until their body slows down.

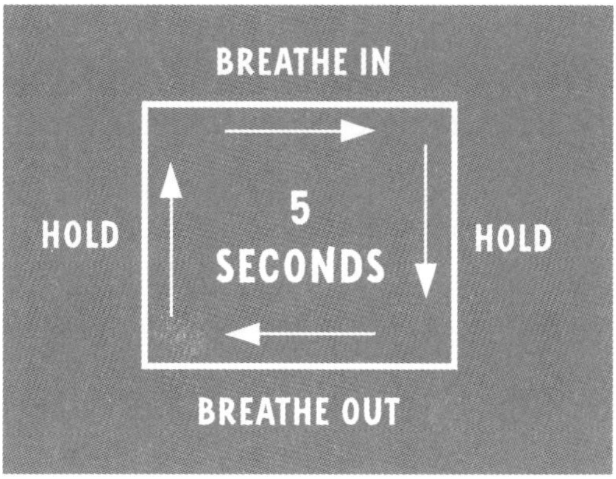

ENVIRONMENTAL SAFETY SKILLS

- *Change of Scenery*: Help the child move to a place where they feel safe. Maybe for one child, this means going outside and taking a walk at a park. For another, it may mean moving to a room that is comforting and quiet. This intervention is especially helpful when someone feels trapped in their thoughts or trapped in the place they're in.
- *Grounding Object/Music/Image/Book/Art:* Are there particular objects, songs, stories, books, or images that your child enjoys? Having these on hand to use or designing them through art forms for times when a child is feeling overwhelmed is another way to create safety. Some of my clients carry a soft stone or putty with them, holding and pressing into it when they feel strong emotions. Others have a playlist of soothing music or storybooks they can read, even just for a few minutes. Others have a scrapbook of images they like to look at.
- *Engaging the Senses*: Similar to 5-4-3-2-1, any efforts to engage a child's senses in the present moment are helpful. You can use things like a frozen orange or lemon, an ice pack, or a heating pad for this. Engaging the senses will activate the part of the brain that allows humans to regulate emotion and calm down.

As we wrap up this chapter, I want to emphasize one final time that, as difficult as this content is to read, it is even more difficult to experience. Too many young children experience abuse and its aftereffects alone. You can be the difference in a child's life by facing these horrors alongside them with tenderness and grace.

CHAPTER 8

"WHAT DO I DO ABOUT SLEEPOVERS OR OVERNIGHT TRIPS?"

PREPARING FOR MOMENTS WHEN YOU AREN'T THERE

If you have a kid who is between four and nine, this chapter can help you build on what you have already learned about developing rules for your family and communicating those rules with others. Perhaps some of you have decided that you won't allow your young child to go on sleepovers and overnight trips without your supervision. If that's the case, parts of this chapter won't apply to you—but it's still valuable for you to think carefully about *why* you have that rule and how to communicate it both to your peers and to your child. Others of you may, for any number of reasons, allow your child to sleep outside of the home without your supervision at times.

Even if you have a general family rule of not doing sleepovers, you might still need to make occasional exceptions to that rule if a younger sibling is born, you are a single parent with prolonged work commitments, you attend a wedding where children are not invited, you go to the hospital, or another emergency situation arises. Regardless of whether sleepovers are a regular occurrence in your family or only happen in occasional emergencies, it's important to think through them as a family.

THINKING THROUGH SLEEPOVERS

Each parent's level of comfort with sleepovers will vary. Some agree only to sleepovers with certain trusted family or friends. Others make a strict "no sleepover" rule. Still others have an age when they begin to allow sleepovers, much like some families have an age when they begin allowing a personal phone. Regardless, the principles in this section are critical to keep in mind in preparing for the eventual possibility of a sleepover.

WHEN SLEEPOVERS ARE NOT ALLOWED

If your family has a "no sleepover" rule, this can provide an extra layer of security for your child as well as creating some challenges. Maybe you have found that your child doesn't need to sleep outside of your home to build strong connections with friends. While there are some social costs to a "no sleepovers" rule—especially as children get older and receive invitations to group parties that involve sleepovers—this rule can also be an opportunity to build a child's confidence in their ability to "do things differently" than their peers and still be liked and respected. Certainly, immature kids who pick on your child for not being allowed to sleep over at a friend's home should not be the gauge of your house rules. Not allowing sleepovers helps to protect your child against potentially dangerous situations.

If your child is like most children, they will question this rule at some point. Let's imagine your child asks, "Why can't I sleep over at my cousin's house? Other cousins get to, and I don't like that you always pick me up instead of letting me stay."

First, validate your child's feelings: "It makes sense that you feel disappointed that you can't sleep at your cousin's. It's hard when others do things as a group that we don't do. We can feel left out when that happens, and so I am grateful you are telling me how you are feeling about it."

Second, offer to explain: "Would you like me to explain why we do it that way?"

If your child says yes, keep it simple for a younger child. You don't want to cloud their mind with too much fear about the possible dangers of sleepovers. You can say, "We have found that, even though it's hard to not be at sleepovers, it's best for kids to sleep in your own bed at night.

At sleepovers, kids can stay up too late and wake up cranky the next day. You might not have all the things you need and not be comfortable, and many kids end up calling their parents wanting to go home because it's hard going to sleep in someone else's house. So we decided that, in our family, we would not do sleepovers. Do you have more questions about it?"

If your child wants to know more, you could add, "It's your mom's/dad's job to keep you safe. It's hard for us to keep you safe at night if we aren't in the same place. As you get older, and especially when you are a grown-up, you get to learn how to keep yourself safe without us there all the time. But for now, it's our job to help with that, and this is one way we try to help. So we decided it's best to have this rule for now." You can also offer to help your child figure out how to handle moments when they feel isolated and like they don't belong: "Would it help if we talk about how to respond if your cousins give you a hard time for not sleeping over?"

If your house rules include "no sleepovers," see if your child can internalize this rule as a good thing for them, rather than seeing it as something negative to push back against. If they can find a benefit to sleeping in their own home, that will be ideal. Ask them, "Can you think of any good parts about sleeping at your house at night?" If they can't come up with any, say, "Some kids like to sleep in their own bed because it's more comfy. Other kids like to have a parent if they need something in the middle of the night, and other kids like to know someone is home if they have a bad dream." If, for example, your child says that they do prefer to sleep in their own bed, encourage them to say to a friend, "I sleep best when I sleep in my own bed at night, so I don't mind going home. All I am missing out on is sleeping!" If they do wish they could sleep over, they could also say to their friend, "I wish I could sleep over, too, but it's part of my family rules." The key is helping a child learn to set boundaries for themselves and to abide by their family rules, even when they want two things at the same time (such as a good night's sleep and time with friends).

WHEN SLEEPOVERS ARE ALLOWED

If you are going to allow your child to have sleepovers or will occasionally need someone other than a parent to watch them overnight, I recommend picking a few individuals and / or families you would allow to watch your child overnight.

Maybe you have in-laws or other family close by where you live. Or maybe there are friends who function as family for you. You might want to identify one other backup option, so that if your first choice isn't available, you have another plan already in place.

Whether you have decided to allow sleepovers with one family or several, take a look at the "Sleepover Prep" list. It offers some questions and considerations before making plans for a sleepover. It will also help you identify the qualities you are looking for in people you would allow to watch your kids overnight. You can't prepare for everything, but you can prepare for some things. Sleepovers is one of them!

SLEEPOVER PREP

Questions to ask yourself:

- How long have I known this person/family?
- How well do I know and trust the adult(s) caring for my child?
- How well does my child know and trust the adult(s) caring for them?
- Does this person/family have similar house rules?
- Do these adults, and the children living in their home, support our family rules when they are with our children? Or are they known for undermining our family rules and doing things outside of what we support?
- Is my child able to speak up if something happens that they don't like (both in general and specifically with this person/family)?
- Am I available to pick up my child if they need something or feel uncomfortable, or will I be unreachable? Who could my child call if I was not available?
- Topics to talk about with your child:

- Remind them about body boundaries: No one can touch them without their permission.
- Remind them about privacy when changing, bathing, and going to the bathroom.
- Plan to check in over the course of the evening at least one time. This can be a text or phone call.
- Decide on a word to use if the child feels unsafe and wants to be picked up. If they say the word or phrase in a phone call, let them know you will come pick them up immediately.
- Remind your child that they can come home if they would like, and they would never be forced to stay if they are not comfortable.

Questions to ask the other adult(s)/family:

- "Will you be home to supervise?"
- "Will you be leaving the children with someone else for any part of the sleepover?"
- "Who else will be in the home at the time of the sleepover?" (This includes older children, other friends, or other extended family members.)
- "Can my child use your phone to text or call? We always check in at least once during sleepovers."

Imagine you're talking with a close family friend or extended family member to ask them your "Sleepover Prep" questions. Here's a good way to begin that conversation:

> "I wanted to call you and touch base about the invitation for Cassandra to come over for a sleepover. She would love to come—thanks so much for the invitation. We don't always do sleepovers in our family, but when we do, we want to make sure we have an open conversation with the adults in the home beforehand. I just wanted to run a few questions by you, if that's okay with you. It's just our standard way of doing things in our house."

DEFINING AND IDENTIFYING DISCOMFORT

As your child starts venturing out of the home more often, it's crucial that they're able to identify their own discomfort and know how to handle it. What does discomfort feel like? This is an important word for a child to know and be able to identify in themselves. We can teach this concept to children in tangible ways, helping them learn that, once they identify their discomfort, they can communicate it to others.

Let's imagine your eight-year-old child is going away to a weeklong summer camp that is not overnight. A week or so before camp, you could take them out for a special treat or a walk around the park. At some point, begin to ask them how they are feeling about their camp. You can bring up scenarios they may encounter and ask how they want to handle those scenarios. You could ask things like, "If you see one kid picking on another kid, what would you do about it?" You could also ask, "If a new kid comes up to you whom you haven't met, what could you say to get to know them?" These are some simple questions to get a conversation going.

Then you could say this to give them greater understanding about how to identify and respond to discomfort:

> "Honey, sometimes new experiences can be exciting and also uncomfortable. Do you know what uncomfortable feels like? [Pause for answer.] Being uncomfortable can feel like a lot of different things. It can feel like a headache or stomachache, butterflies in our stomach, or tightness in our chest. It can feel like a rubber band being stretched out, like being stuck in the mud, or like having tingling feelings in our hands. It can make our hands shake, and our voice can get quiet or shaky. These are all normal signs of feeling uncomfortable or nervous. You may feel uncomfortable while you're at camp because it's new. That's normal, and you can do things that feel new and uncomfortable.
>
> "But sometimes, at camps or school or playdates, things happen that are not okay, and they can make us feel very uncomfortable. It's like a flashing red light: our body's way of telling us something is wrong, asking us to pay attention! An example of this would be if a person asks you to show them your penis/breasts/butt or tries to show you theirs,

or touches your body in the areas that are private. Other times, it's a flashing yellow light: something is happening, we aren't sure what it is, but it feels weird and confusing to us. That's what can happen when a person teases us or says a joke we don't like. We also want to pay attention to this, even if we aren't sure yet what it means.

"So, if you get that 'flashing red light' feeling, right away you can go find an adult whom you trust. Ask them to call me. Let's plan a code phrase you could say when you call me, like 'I want to go to the zoo instead of this camp.' If it's a 'flashing yellow light' feeling, you can always wait until the end of the day to tell me what happened. Then we can figure out what to do about it. We don't want to ignore the feelings in our body. We want to pay attention, okay?"

FOLLOWING UP

Let's say that the weeklong day camp has ended. The whole week has gone by, and your child said nothing about feeling uncomfortable throughout the week. There were no "flashing red light" or "flashing yellow light" moments. You could easily assume that everything went well and leave it at that. After all, you're busy with so many things as a parent. You may even think, "We talked about it. If something happened, they would have told me!"

Your assumption may be correct, especially if you have very open lines of communication with your child. But it's still valuable to check in—especially if you're in the process of building better communication with your child or developing your own confidence in these conversations.

Here's one way you could circle back. In a moment of relaxation and reflection, such as when you're driving in the car or winding down for bed, say something like this: "I've been meaning to ask a bit more about your camp. I know you told me about it some already, and I'm so glad it was so fun for you! I also wanted to ask about the 'flashing red light' and 'flashing yellow light' moments we talked about. Do you remember what those mean?"

If a child says no, briefly remind them: "Flashing red is when your body is telling you something is wrong, and flashing yellow is when your body is saying that something feels strange or confusing and to pay attention!"

Then ask, "What were some 'flashing yellow light' moments this week?" Instead of saying, "Did you have any 'flashing yellow light' moments?" assume they did have some! The more open-ended your question is, the better. You may be surprised what you learn, and it can help you know the types of things that can come up for a child that they may need your help making sense of after the fact.

After that conversation, ask about "flashing red light" moments. Ask, "What 'flashing red light' moments did you have?" If nothing horrific happened, that's good news! It doesn't mean it wasn't worth having the conversation. It means you're opening the door for open dialogue now and in the future. Also, it lets you relate to your child, not only in crisis moments that we spoke about in chapter 7, but in the ebbs and flows of their daily lives.

ANTICIPATING QUESTIONS ABOUT SEX

As children begin to interact with other children and adults in school, at playdates, on sleepovers, and elsewhere, you can expect them to overhear conversations about sex. In a perfect world, children would quickly bring these concepts up with parents after they hear about them. In an imperfect world, there are all kinds of barriers to this. A child might not want to be seen as a tattletale or to get someone in trouble. Maybe they feel as if they should already know what another person is talking about when they use the word "sex" or other words like it.

No matter how a child thinks about the moments when they hear the word "sex" for the first time, often they will have already asked you, "Where do babies come from?" or some rendition of that question. The problem is, if you signal when you answer that question that you are uncomfortable with it—or that it is silly or weird, or that your kid is too young for it—they are less likely to circle back in the future.

I want you to be the primary person your child goes to with these kinds of questions, and initiating proactive conversations will allow you to be an initial source of knowledge and support. So let's plan for how you can initiate teachable moments about procreation. (If your child hasn't asked yet, but is stepping into environments where he or she is around a lot of other children, you can expect it has likely already popped up in conversation or in their mind.) Try capitalizing on times when you are visiting a new baby or expecting a baby in the family by asking, "Do you ever wonder where babies come from?" This timing will let you shape the conversation and prevent your child from first receiving sex education from other kids without you present.

HOW DO WE EXPLAIN WHERE BABIES COME FROM?

When you initiate this conversation or this question is brought up by your child, how do you want to expand on it? For a younger child, around three or four, you may simply say, "I'm so grateful we can talk about this! It's such a good question. A mom and dad help create a baby, and it is such a beautiful thing parents get to do." If the child is wanting to know more, you could add, "It is the coolest thing. Babies are created by God, with a mom and dad's help. They grow in a mom's uterus, which is right here [pointing to your abdominal area]. The uterus keeps the baby safe until the baby is ready to come out."

Let's imagine your child is extra inquisitive. They want to know even more. So you continue:

> "You know how some creatures hatch from an egg (birds, frogs, alligators) and some are born from their mom (dogs, cats)? A human baby is born from their mom. Humans are made from something called an egg from their mom and something called a sperm from their dad. When the egg and the sperm join, and God places a soul there, a baby's life begins. A man provides the sperm, a woman provides the egg, and God provides the soul. Isn't that amazing?"

The key is to communicate what you know without embarrassment or awkwardness. Some of it will likely go over a three-year-old's head, which is okay—the important thing is that this conversation will signal to your child that you are the person to ask about such things.[2]

Some readers may be wondering, "Should we really say words like 'uterus,' 'sperm,' and 'egg'?" The answer is yes. Remember how we talked in chapter 2 about the value of using medical terms for genitalia and other anatomy? These terms build on one another to make sense of the human body in all its beauty. Laying a foundation now by using words like 'uterus,' 'egg,' and 'ovaries' will make talking about menstrual periods and fertility so much easier later on. Similarly for boys, using words like 'penis' and 'sperm' will make talking about nocturnal emissions (also known as wet dreams) and erections so much easier as they enter puberty. We will talk more about how to prepare a junior-high- or high-school-aged child for puberty in book 2, so hang tight for that. But trust me, a period will be much less scary if your daughter knows ahead of time where the menstrual blood is coming from and what it is telling her about her body! A noticeable erection or nocturnal emission will be much less confusing if your son can talk to you about it openly and understand the anatomy that contributes to this.

Long before we get to periods and such, a child will at some point want to know how a mom and dad help create a baby. Communicating what I shared above can give you a solid starting point. Remember, it is not disgusting to talk about how babies are made, even if you haven't had models for how to do it without blushing. The truth is, the reality of sexual intercourse and the unity and potential for new life are all beautiful, willed by God, and for our good and the good of society, if we have eyes to see it. Let's help our kids see it!

A simple way to gauge how much detail your child is ready for in conversations about sex is to provide just a few pieces of information at a time and then ask, "Do you have any more questions?" If your child says no, no need to go deeper for now. But by asking this follow-up question, you're showing your child that you are the one whom they can come back to, again and again, as they want to learn more. This is all the more important once kids start to hear about sex and procreation from others. If you've handled the last conversation with them well, and then asked if they have more questions in order to show that you're willing to share more with them, they're more likely to come back to you when new questions do arise.

HOW DO WE TALK ABOUT CHILDREN?

In addition to shaping how our children think and talk about sex, we also want to help shape how our children think and talk about younger children as they grow up, including the prospect that they might also one day be called by God to raise children of their own. Just as our kids are eventually bound to hear other people talk about sex when we're not around, they're also guaranteed to hear people talk about giving birth to and raising kids. How do we want to shape our children's understanding of child-raising?

We live in a society that sometimes views the ability to raise one's own children as a civil right, yet also negatively describes the experience of parenting as a burden or even "a death sentence." While the idea that children are a burden is sometimes communicated subtly, it can be quite blatant at other times. As you begin having conversations with your kid about how babies are made, this also creates an opportunity to share what Christians believe about the value of children.

I grew up as an older child in a large Catholic family. Other adults would frequently ask me and my siblings, "Are your parents done?" Their tone said it all. They clearly thought that my parents *should* be done. Even as a young child, I would ask myself, "What's so bad about kids—what's so bad about me and my siblings—that makes everyone hope my parents are done having kids?"

If you have a lot of kids—or if you're planning on it eventually—I'd recommend coming up with one or two creative and kind ways for your kids to respond to questions like these. If you aren't sure if your kids have already been asked this question, you can start by finding out:

"Do people ever ask you if Mom and Dad are done having kids? How do you respond? What is that like for you?"

Once you know whether this has already happened, you can help your child come up with a few quick ways to respond. Remind your child that they don't always have to respond, but at least they'll have things they could say if they would like to. They can try a warm and sincere response, a direct and more serious response, or a playful, silly one:

- "We are wonderful, why would they want to be done?"
- "They don't really talk to me about that."
- "After twenty more, I think they will be!"

You might have also experienced other adults speaking negatively to you about kids in the hearing of your own kids. For example, someone might meet all your kids and then say, "You have your hands full," in a tone that signals the thing your hands are full of is *not* a good thing. Keep in mind in those moments that the children are listening, and their understanding of what it means to raise children is being shaped by what you say. What you may intend as a harmless joke can stick with a kid longer than you realize. Look for creative ways to communicate your kids' value and worth in response to these moments, and work hard not to say such things in the future, even if you've said them before.

On the other hand, some families are smaller for various reasons, including infertility and health issues. Teaching children about those cases as well prepares them for the possibility that children may not come easily for every Catholic family, and families can look different. Some may have one child. Other families have children through adoption or fostering. Helping kids understand this can help them value the beautiful gift of children and view families big and small without judgment.

Also, if a child in a small family asks for a sibling, it is important for the child to know that a sibling would be a wonderful gift, but also if it cannot happen, they are enough and loved.

Raising children who understand that they are valued as a gift is no small thing. This sets a framework for them to know their dignity and worth and offer others that same treatment. Even more significant, it sets a framework for them to know their belovedness in the eyes of God. There is no more important task than helping a child see themselves as loved and wanted, rebuking any messaging that does harm to their understanding of their value and worth.

WHAT DO WE SAY WHEN WE SEE ERECTIONS?

Erections can occur in boys as early as the third trimester of fetal development, and they will persist after birth and throughout childhood.[3]

Abnormal erections in children are those that last longer than an hour, are consistently painful, or when the penis is red, swollen, or showing a rash. Be sure to consult with your doctor immediately if this is the case. Outside of that, there is no need to worry when you notice an erection in a child. Still, it is a valuable opportunity for a conversation.

We can distinguish between erections that occur prior to puberty and those that occur at puberty, because the erections that occur at puberty can lead to ejaculation, whereas those earlier will not.[4] Some boys may feel afraid when they see an erection or may report pain when it occurs. If this is the case, you can help your son take a bath to relax or change his pants to looser clothing.[5] Both of these can make the discomfort less intense. But first, you will want to describe in simple terms what is happening.

Here's how you might approach a conversation about erections when you or your child notices it:

> "Do you notice that your penis is sticking up? That is a normal thing that happens to boys. It will go back down on its own. If it ever stays up a really long time or hurts you, please let me know. Do you have any questions? Remember, your penis is a private area, which means you do not show it to others, even when it is sticking out like that, and you do not let others touch it. You also don't touch it in front of people. It is important to protect and take care of your penis because, like every other part of your body, it is a gift."

If your child was to ask you why an erection happens, try saying this:

> "Sometimes an erection happens for no reason, and other times it happens from touching it because your penis fills with blood in those moments. As you get older, we can talk more about it too. There is no need to be afraid of it when it happens. If you ever have questions or hear things from other people about erections, we can talk about that, okay? There is so much to learn about your body, and it is such a gift from God!"

HOW DO WE HELP KIDS RESPOND TO CRASS TALK?

One of the biggest benefits of talking with your kids about sex before they hear it from others is that you get to prepare them to identify and respond to inappropriate talk about sex. Being proactive is always better than being reactive. Yes, even a five-year-old can identify inappropriate talk, and even a five-year-old can learn what to say in response.

Francine, a five-year-old girl, was at her same-aged friend Shawn's house for a playdate. They were joined by three neighborhood friends who were six, seven, and nine. While she was playing with the boys, she started to hear them talk about their "dicks." She intuitively knew that what they were saying was not appropriate talk. She didn't have all the words to explain this, but when her mom picked her up and asked her how the playdate was, Francine said, "I don't like Shawn's neighbors. I don't like what they were saying to me. They kept saying yucky words."

What does it look like for Francine's mom to respond?

Francine's mom can start by commending Francine for listening to her gut: "I am so proud of you for paying attention when you felt uncomfortable."

Then she can ask a follow-up question using Francine's own words: "Do you want to tell me the yucky words they were saying? You don't have to if it makes you uncomfortable. You could write it down if you don't want to say it, or you could just tell me more about what happened next." Some kids will not want to share what was said. That's okay. It's not necessary in this context to get all of the details. What is more important is being able to validate the discomfort and celebrate Francine's growing ability to speak up for herself.

Once Francine's mom hears the context, she can validate the thoughts and feelings Francine had. "You didn't like what they were saying because what they were saying wasn't okay. I'm so proud of you for noticing that and telling me. I would have felt disgusted and frustrated, too, when they said something yucky."

Then she can help Francine learn how to respond. "Sometimes people say things about their bodies or other people's bodies that are not okay. You can always tell me. You can also ignore them, walk away like you did, change the topic, or speak up if you want to. Should we come up with a plan of what you could say if you decide to speak up?"

Here are a few responses Francine's mom could suggest to Francine for next time:

- "Please stop talking that way. I don't want to hear that."
- "If you don't stop talking that way, I am leaving."
- "It's called a penis. Why are you calling it that and talking about it so much? It's really not cool or funny."

These one-liners might come in handy for Francine in future years. What a gift to help your kids stock their conversational "toolbox" for whatever inappropriate talk and behavior comes their way.

CHAPTER 9

"HOW DO I TALK WITH MY CHILD ABOUT GENDER AND SAME-SEX SEXUALITY?"

ASSISTING A CHILD IN UNDERSTANDING LGBTQ-RELATED QUESTIONS

Let's turn now to another common question I get from Christian parents and teachers who want to learn how to answer children's questions about sexual orientation and gender. I've written other books about gender and how to accompany a loved one or client experiencing gender-related distress, but those in-depth resources are primarily for engaging in conversation with teens and young adult children who are exploring their own gender.[1] How should you talk about gender, and also about sexual orientation, with kids who are simply asking curious questions or trying to make sense of things they've heard from their friends?

This chapter will help you think about how to frame general conversations along these lines with young children, whereas book 2 of this series will tackle more specific conversations about sexual orientation and gender with teens in your life.

There are lots of pieces involved in your early conversations with younger children about these topics: How can I create a healthy home environment for my child to come to me with questions about sexual orientation and gender? What is the best way to respond when a child brings up questions about this? What do I do if my child asks me about their friend's sexual orientation or gender-related questions, or about things they hear about LGBTQ experiences in school or on media? Perhaps most significantly, what if I start to suspect that my young child might grow up to be attracted to the same sex, or that they're already experiencing distress related to their gender?

In this chapter, I'll begin by reflecting on some of the challenges we face as Christians in engaging these conversations proactively. I'll offer some guidance for parents who have a child wrestling with gender-related distress, as well as for parents fielding questions about gender and sexuality when your child isn't personally experiencing this. (In book 2, I'll also offer guidance for parents whose kids experience attraction to the same sex; but since sexual attraction more often enters the picture at or after puberty, that conversation can wait, whereas some kids as young as three or four years old will experience gender-related distress.) I'll close with a few words about how to respond to information children find in books, or on social media, or through friends to help you better engage and invite conversation with your kids.

A REFLECTION ON CULTURE: CHALLENGES AND AN OPPORTUNITY

When I tell people that my specialty as a psychologist lies at the intersection of religious faith and sexuality and gender, people react in a variety of ways. Some are confused and skeptical about how these things can coexist: "How does that work with being a Christian?" Others are curious: "I want to hear more about what that looks like. It's such an important area." Others show anger, fear, and disgust: "I don't know how you do that. I can't stand those people. Isn't it terrifying what they are trying to teach our kids?" Others poke fun at people who identify as LGBTQ: "Oh, gosh. I identify as a bird, so I need your help."

If you have concerns about how shifting Western understandings of sexual orientation and gender will impact our children, specifically elementary-school-aged kids, you are not alone. Pope Francis has written more than once about this complexity, discussing the concerns he holds about ideologically driven perspectives on gender that differ significantly from a Catholic vision of the human person.[2] Other Christians have also written about their concerns with how current gender paradigms contrast a Christian vision for gender.[3] I, too, hold concerns about the rising number of people treating gender as nothing more than a social construct. I'm especially concerned about the impact this narrative will have on children over time, including messaging that portrays the binary of male and female as merely oppressive.

At the same time, I'm also concerned by some of the statements I hear being made about LGBTQ-identified people by Christian communities. Our children are listening not only to the words we say about others but also to the tone we adopt as we speak. They will gauge by both tone and content whether we *really* believe each person, without exception, is made in the image and likeness of God. If we speak condescendingly, mockingly, and dismissively in our conversations about sex and gender paradigms we disagree with—and, more importantly, about the people who are compelled by these paradigms—our children will likely assume any number of problematic things.

They may conclude that holding historically Christian views on sexuality and gender is incompatible with Christian love, feeling that they need to abandon these views in order to truly love their LGBTQ-identified friends. Or they may conclude that Christians do not need to treat those with whom we disagree with respect and charity, and they may follow in our mocking footsteps. Neither of these outcomes is a victory for Christianity. We do not need to abandon historic Christian views, and we also do not need more generations of Christians conveying harmful, cruel things about people who identify as LGBTQ. Most of all, we do not need more children to be bullied in our schools and communities for experiencing same-sex sexuality or gender-related distress.[4] The *Catechism of the Catholic Church* is clear that "every sign of unjust discrimination" regarding sexual minorities "should be avoided."[5] We can help our children be people who speak up against bullying.

Christians today have many opportunities to offer a distinctively Christian response when LGBTQ-related questions arise. One valuable opportunity we have is the chance to show by our tone, our actions, and our conversations that we really do profess that each person carries a fundamental dignity—especially those we disagree with. Yet this process is by no means easy, especially when our emotions are running high. I want to invite you to step into this conversation with an awareness of what your own emotions are when you try to approach the topic of LGBTQ experiences. Notice your feelings, validate them as important to pay attention to, and let's find a way to acknowledge these feelings without letting fear drive your parenting.

MOVING BEYOND FEAR-BASED PARENTING

We need nuance and peace to position ourselves as a resource to young children about such important and complex topics as human sexuality and gender. Not only that, but we also want to create inviting spaces in our homes for children to see us as a resource as they move into their teen years. In adolescence and early adulthood, every person will face questions about identity, friendship, sexual behavior, romantic relationships, and cultivating healthy intimacy. I want your children to know they can bring you in as a reliable guide, both now and later. However you speak about sexuality and gender now (and especially if you say nothing), your child is listening and gauging whether or not they ought to share such things with you as they grow up.

In my experience, many well-intentioned Christian parents relate to young children in fear-based ways when it comes to sexuality and gender. For example, a parent operating out of fear might refuse to allow a little boy to have playdates with little girls or cultivate his interest in art, cooking, and theater, out of concern that these activities will "make him gay." They might restrict a little girl's access to certain sports because "every girl on my high school softball team was a lesbian," or they might cut off connections with any LGBTQ-identified family members in the hopes that doing so will restrict access to "bad influences" on their children.[6]

When you parent out of fear, this is likely to signal unintentionally to your child that you're too fragile to receive their questions. There is also no evidence that fear-based parenting strategies "prevent" certain manifestations of sexual orientation or gender questions. What they do instead is isolate children from bringing these conversations up with parents as they get older. Many children will read the room and gauge that they ought to keep such questions to themselves.

In fact, when it comes to Christian young people who experience attraction to the same sex, many will keep their experience of attraction to themselves for several years after their first awareness of it.[7] This means they are left to navigate their attractions—and their questions about those attractions—alone. This is a recipe for shame in children. Frankly, it also increases the likelihood that they will channel their curiosity about their attraction through early sexual behaviors and pornography. Not only that, but it limits the opportunity you have as parents to teach sexual stewardship in your children.[8]

THINGS TO AVOID WITH YOUR CHILD[9]

- Causing physical harm to a child who behaves in ways that aren't typical of their gender
- Name-calling or being verbally aggressive toward a child who doesn't conform to gender expectations
- Isolating a child from family events
- Blaming a child for bullying or harassment they encounter because of their gender nonconformity
- Pressuring a child to engage in gender-typical behaviors that are rooted in stereotypes
- Telling a child that God will punish a person because of their sexual attraction or gender questioning (i.e., "You will go to hell if . . .")
- Communicating that you would be ashamed of your child if they were to experience same-sex sexual attraction or gender questions
- Shunning a person whom a child knows to be a sexual or gender minority
- Telling a child not to admit their questions about sexuality and gender, so that the child is left to explore sexuality and/or gender without support

Holding in mind what *not* to do, I want us to identify proactive ways to create trusting and secure spaces for kids to be able to open up about their experiences and questions surrounding sexuality and gender. We can begin by gaining knowledge about these topics, including making sure that we understand key terms related to sexuality and gender.

KEY TERMS

Words matter. So often in conversations about sexuality and gender, we aren't quite sure what we are talking about, and this can make it confusing from the start. Because of this, let's begin by defining our terms.[10]

KEY TERMS

- Biological sex: The traits—such as chromosomes, genes, hormones, and physical markers—that distinguish males and females.
- Gender: The psychological, social, and cultural aspects of being a man or a woman.
- Gender identity: A range of labels that a person may identify with in light of their internal experience of gender, especially when it might depart from their sex.[11]
- Gender dysphoria: The experience of clinically-significant distress related to having a psychological and emotional gender that does not match one's biological sex.
- Transgender: An umbrella term for the many ways people might experience, present, express, or live out their gender differently from people whose sense of gender is congruent with their biological sex.
- Disorders of sex development/Intersex: A term for diverse "medical conditions that involve the reproductive systems and refer to atypical development of anatomic, gonadal, and/or chromosomal sex." Some people may become aware of these disorders at birth and others may not become aware until the time of puberty or encountering difficulties having biological children later in life.[12]

- Sexual attraction/desire: The most descriptive way to describe the direction of sexual and romantic desire, which can be toward men, women, or both.
- Sexual orientation: The enduring pattern and direction of a person's attractions, specifically when these attractions persist in strength over time. This category includes words such as heterosexual, straight, bisexual, same-sex attracted, gay, and lesbian to describe one's orientation.
- Sexual identity: The way in which a person may communicate their sexual attractions and sexual orientation as an aspect of identity to others through various labels. This can include terms such as "heterosexual," "straight," "bisexual," "same-sex attracted," "gay," or "lesbian." Some will use these words to indicate that their sexual orientation is integral to their identity, and others will use one of these words as an adjective to describe an aspect of their experience. The *Catechism of the Catholic Church* and various encyclicals define "sexual identity" as one's identity as man or woman, rather than defining it in terms of patterns of sexual desire and the ways people may identify as a result of these patterns. I give you the above definition of sexual identity in order to account for the common way people may use the term "sexual identity" in informal conversation, since so often parents may be confused with a different use of this term than what they have read in Church documents.[13]
- Sexual minority: This is a term that can be applied to a person who, by virtue of their pattern of sexual attraction, is in a numerical minority. It is an umbrella term that can be broad enough to account for all people whose experience of attraction is non-heterosexual, without assuming every person with a sexual minority experience identifies as lesbian, gay, or bisexual.

Most people's pattern of attraction is exclusively toward the opposite sex.[14] Likewise, most people's gender aligns with their biological sex. (For example, most people who are born male experience themselves as a man.) But just as there are some people who find themselves attracted to the same sex, there are also some people whose experience of their gender does not align with their biological sex.

When I distinguish between biological sex and gender, that doesn't mean that I'm assuming gender can be completely detached from biological sex. Rather, using language that distinguishes these two concepts helps us account for the experience of some Christians for whom these two aspects of self are in conflict, and Catholic teaching indicates sex and gender can be distinguished but not separated.[15] While the distinction between the two might seem irrelevant when a person's sex and gender are in alignment, it can be helpful to name them separately when a person's gender and their biological sex are not in alignment, and especially when they are in painful conflict.

More broadly, if you feel hesitation about using language that originated in or has been co-opted into a secular paradigm, take time to listen to why other people have found it helpful before you reject it outright. We can sometimes use terms as tools to help us find nuance and convey information about different experiences of gender and sexual desire, without subscribing to the philosophical assumptions of any term completely. We do this often with language, actually, and this is no exception.

WHAT DO WE DO WHEN OUR CHILD EXPERIENCES CONFLICT AROUND THEIR BIOLOGICAL SEX?[16]

It has been a true gift to meet with many Christian parents who have a young child navigating life with significant pain around their gender. The psychological term for this experience is "gender dysphoria": a person feels a fundamental conflict between their biological sex and their gender. This means that, while they may "know" cognitively that they are born male or female, they experience themselves as the opposite sex and demonstrate significant gender atypicality in their interests, dress, behaviors, and even their experience of their genitalia.

Gender dysphoria doesn't merely describe a young girl who enjoys playing with trucks and hates Barbies, or a young boy who likes to try on his mother's high heels. Gender dysphoria involves a mental-health concern that can range in intensity, severity, and the degree to which it negatively impacts a person's quality of life. Like any other mental-health concern, it can be hard (though not impossible) to understand it if you have not known someone struggling with it or struggled with it yourself. Humility is important here, and mockery does no one any good in this space.

UNDERSTANDING GENDER DEVELOPMENT

For all of us, our sense of gender begins to show up between ages two and five. For example, one young child I know started to notice, right around age three, that people told her she looked like her dad. She started telling her parents and others that she was a boy, reasoning that because she looked like her dad, she must be a boy. After one or two conversations in which her parents explained that she was still a girl even though she looked more like her dad (in the sense that she had his eyes, his hair color, and a similar personality to him), she did what most kids do. She started to tell people, "I'm a girl," and that was that.

For kids with what is called "early onset gender dysphoria," the gender-related pain can show up as early as between two and five. Instead of the story I told above, in which a child gains and loses her gender questions very quickly, a young girl with early onset gender dysphoria might have a persistent sense that they *really are* a boy, even though they were born a girl. If you're a parent whose child has this experience, I am so grateful you are reading. I know this can be an incredibly challenging journey, and few people understand the intricacies of your situation.

FINDING CONCRETE SUPPORTS

I remember meeting with one Catholic couple whose six-year-old, Dylan, showed signs of significant distress about gender. Dylan was in Catholic school and loved so much of it. At the same time, the school didn't seem to know what to do with Dylan. The parents got the sense that, if Dylan continued to struggle with gender-related distress, the school would expect them to pull Dylan out. They didn't want to send Dylan to a non-Catholic school, because their faith was important to their family, but at the same time, they were worried that Dylan would experience bullying as he got older, and they felt unsure of what to do.

If this is your story, here are some principles and guides for accompanying your child:

- Seek mental-health care from a balanced and competent mental-health professional who can provide guidance for you in your parenting and support for your child.[17]
- Be patient with yourself and with your child. Resist the temptation to jump to hasty conclusions in any direction.[18]
- Do not blame yourself for your child's gender-related distress. We do not fully know what causes gender incongruence, and beating yourself up for it will not help you be present for your child.
- Help your child cultivate their interests, talents, and gifts, and bolster their sense of worth and value, without fixating on their gender identity at the expense of their personhood.
- Help your child know about both God's unconditional love for them and your unconditional love for them. Be sure they know that their pain about gender does not preclude them from a relationship with Christ; he cares about their particular challenges and has created them for a life of thriving.

It is also so helpful for a child to know they are not alone in their experience of dysphoria. This can help reduce the sense of isolation. Let's turn to a practical way to communicate this truth to your child:

> "Honey, I can tell it is hard for you that you weren't born a _____. You wish you were, don't you? I want you to know that you are not alone in this. There are other kids like you who grow up to be healthy and holy adults. We will find a path that helps you get there too. God loves you, and I love you, and he will help you with this."

LIMIT-SETTING

There may also be times with a small child when you need to set limits around their clothing choices for their safety. This is especially true for families with a child who experiences gender distress. For example, let's say that your six-year-old male child wants to wear a dress to church on Sunday, because he has play dresses that he likes to try on sometimes when playing with his friends. You could respond by saying, "Play clothes are okay in the home, but not in church." This is just like what you do when you have certain toys that are "indoor toys" and others that are "outdoor toys."

The key to limit-setting is to focus your rules around what kind of clothing is appropriate in different settings—the kind of rules you would set for any child—rather than inventing rules that apply only to your child who is struggling with their gender. We do not want to unintentionally shame a child for their interests and preferences. In fact, efforts to shame or restrict their access to their interests can actually make a child's gender-related distress worse. Limit-setting is valuable in parenting your young child, but it is most effective when it's done tactfully and in a non-shaming way.

RESPONDING TO CONCERNED ADULTS

One of the biggest challenges for many parents is learning to respond to the unsolicited opinions and critiques of others. I often hear parents who are *not* in another parent's shoes say critically, "If that were my child . . ." I want to gently remind parents who are inclined to say these things that, at the end of the day, you really can't know exactly what you would do if you were in another person's shoes.

Oversimplifying another family's situation and giving unsolicited advice helps no one. It can often feel patronizing and minimizing of the complex questions parents face. If you're an outsider who wants to offer a parent advice, a good practice is to ask permission first: "Would it help if I gave my perspective, or would it be better if I listen to you for now?" If you are a parent on the receiving end of unsolicited advice, it might help to communicate directly what you need: "What I am needing right now is [support, a listening ear, tangible advice]." After all, people will not always know what you are needing. As a parent, being able to be direct about what you need may save you a lot of frustration in the long run.

In the case of parents with a child wrestling with gender distress, being direct about what your needs are—and responding to unsolicited advice—can be especially difficult and especially important. If a loved one, teacher, or friend expresses concern about how you are caring for your child who is wrestling with their gender, try saying, "Thank you for sharing that. We are doing the best we can with our situation and would ask for your prayers and your respect for our privacy in this time."

When people ask how they can help, you could also say: "I appreciate your offering to help. We hope you can understand that we are already getting support for this, and so advice-giving from others is not as helpful. For now, what you could do is keep this information private and please speak up if our child's difficulties become a topic of gossip in the [church/school]. That's how you can best help our family, and we would be so grateful for it."

Not everyone deserves or has a right to your family's private information and wrestling. This is especially true when the information regards something as intimate as your child's experience of distress around their gender. I hope you feel permission to keep the information safeguarded and to tell others on a need-to-know basis, knowing that gossip in families and communities can do more harm to everyone involved.

If you're a parent raising a child with gender-related distress, the already-challenging task of parenting will likely have additional layers of challenge. Some people might assume that you're too permissive, that you're rejecting Christian teaching, or make other assumptions about your family. Others may assume that you are a proponent of certain sociopolitical movements and policies because of your family's situation, and they may misunderstand your heart. Still others may criticize you for being, from their perspective, insufficiently supportive of your own child, not knowing the nature of the conversations you're having with them. Take courage in being misunderstood—Christ, too, was misunderstood time and time again in his own mission. Be steadfast in prayer, trusting that God will provide the grace, resourcing, and encouragement you will need for this journey as a family, no matter where it leads.

HOW DO WE PREVENT BULLYING AROUND SEXUALITY OR GENDER?

Bullying and teasing is all too common, and adult sexual and/or gender minorities have often shared with me about how frequent bullying was for them in early childhood. It is all too common for young boys to be mocked and called horrible things when they are friends with girls or don't enjoy rough-and-tumble play. Likewise, young girls often get mocked for doing well in math and science and liking sports such as football. Those remarks can cause a lot of pain and alienation in a small child.

Children who will grow up to experience either same-sex sexuality or gender dysphoria are at greater risk for mental-health concerns such as depression and suicidal thoughts, and bullying and peer rejection can make these mental-health difficulties much more likely.[19] As Christians, we are called to proactively help buffer against the mistreatment of others, and especially those often marginalized. This means raising children who know to stand up against bullying, whenever it occurs, including when it occurs to other kids who may show signs of gender atypicality and/or may experience same-sex attraction as they enter puberty.

Let's take an example of your six-year-old, whom you overhear playing with a group of neighborhood kids in the backyard. As they play, you hear one of the older neighbors, nine-year old Jack, say to one of the other boys, Keegan, "You're a sissy. Stop crying. Only girls cry. Are you a girl?" The first rule of thumb as a parent is to intervene whenever possible in cases of bullying. Step in and say something like this to Jack: "In our house, we don't talk to people that way. Not just girls cry. People who are brave enough to show their feelings cry. If you can't stop talking that way to Keegan, I am going to ask you to leave."

After the fact, try bringing this moment up with your six-year-old:

> "Hey, remember earlier when Jack called Keegan a sissy and made fun of him? That was not okay for him to say. We don't treat people that way. And if you hear someone saying something like that about someone at school, or church, or home, God calls us to speak up. It can be scary to speak up, especially with an older kid, and it's so important to do. What could you say if you hear that again and Mom or Dad isn't around to step in?"

Be sure to coach your child to look the other person straight in the eyes and tell them to stop. If the other person doesn't stop, encourage your child to find a trusted adult. Tell them, "The other kid might tease you if you speak up or tell an adult. That doesn't mean it's the wrong thing to do, but it does mean it's hard to do! Just like Jesus was mocked and teased when he stood up for people who were left out, we can get teased for doing the right thing. Jesus sees your heart and will help you have the courage to speak up." This is one of the best ways to combat bullying: equipping children who witness it to step in.

Many of you have likely already found out how difficult it is to monitor children's safety. You aren't always around in every moment. Many kids will not talk about being teased at school and may think of bullying only as acts of physical violence. This is yet another reason why it's important to proactively anticipate teasing and equip your child to know how to respond and whom to talk to.

For example, here's a conversation you could have with a child who is interested in toys stereotypical for the other sex:

> "I can tell you really like [Barbies/GI Joes/trucks], and I can see why, because they are pretty cool! I love how many interests you have and how confident you are when you play that way. Some kids may wonder why you like those things, and you can tell them that they are just what you like. If kids laugh at you for that or tease you, please tell Mom and Dad. You can always respond by telling them, 'Stop,' or 'Be quiet.' Say it calmly, and they will leave you alone. If they don't, again, please tell me, and we will help.
>
> "Sometimes kids can be mean. They make fun of us for things that are totally okay to like. I used to be made fun of as a kid for liking ____. And I had to learn how to stand up for myself. In our family, we want to teach you how to do that too.
>
> "When people make fun of someone, we can tell them to stop. If they don't listen, we go tell an adult. From time to time, I will ask you about that, but I also hope you can tell me if that is happening to you or your friends. Parents are here to help with those things, and being mean to people is never okay."

HOW DO WE RESPOND TO RESOURCES ABOUT SEXUALITY OR GENDER THAT OUR CHILD SEES IN SCHOOL OR AT THE LIBRARY?

Leann texted me out of the blue. She sent a picture of a book that her seven-year-old son had picked up and read at the school library. The title? *It Feels Good to Be Yourself: A Book about Gender Identity.* She shared, "I have no idea what to say or do. Are there any good resources on how to respond?"

Hopefully this book is one of those good resources! My first response to Leann was to ask, "What reactions and questions did your son have about the book?" Understandably, Leann had not thought to ask her son, because she had panicked. She went back to her son and asked, "What did you think of the book you read about gender?"

Her son said, "I don't know. It was confusing."

Leann responded, "I am so grateful we can talk about it, then. It makes sense that it would be confusing. What questions did you have about it?" Notice that starting the conversation this way enabled Leann to address the questions her son actually had, rather than populating his mind with issues that weren't already there.

Her son's first question was, "Why do some people feel their gender doesn't match their body?"

Here's how a parent could respond to this question:

> "We don't fully know how that happens for some people. Most people, like you, are born a boy and feel like a boy. That's how it is for most kids you will meet. But there are some kids who feel deep pain about not feeling comfortable in their body. And we are a body wherever we go, so that can be really tough for kids, like the ones you read about. Sometimes the boxes our world gives us for what it means to be a boy or a girl can be too small, which makes it harder for all of us, and especially people in this situation."

Leann's son then asked, "Does God love those people?" Here's a good way to respond:

> "Yes, God does love every child, including children who don't feel comfortable in their body. God has a plan for their

> life, like he does for your life and my life. It is definitely a gift when we feel at home in our body, and we can love people who don't have that experience. It's our job to show God's love to everyone by treating them kindly, and that includes the kids you read about in that book."

Leann's son's final question was this: "What if I want to be a boy? Does that book mean I might become a girl someday?"

> "No, that's not what that book means. You are a boy. And you don't have pain around that, and that is a blessing. Your being a boy doesn't change. That can be hard for kids who have gender questions, for sure. Since you don't have those questions, you can be kind and care for people who do. But you don't have to worry about questions that you don't have right now. If those come up, I hope we can talk about it, since our faith can offer us guidance in how to understand God's plan for each of us, including people with gender questions. Okay?"

Here are the major principles to incorporate, which can be applied similarly to a resource a child encounters that has to do with same-sex sexuality or relationships.

- *Ask questions* about your child's gut reactions before giving your reaction to the resource.
- *Validate* your child's reactions: "It makes sense that you felt that way," even if you have a different reaction.
- *Clarify* what questions your child has about the resource. Respond to the actual questions your child has, rather than assuming what they may be wondering.
- *Respond to questions simply and calmly*, by accounting for both the majority experience and the minority experience.
- *Emphasize God's unconditional love* for all people, and the Christian call to reflect that love.
- *Relieve* your child from the need to have to ask questions that are not theirs to ask, or at least not presently on their mind.
- *Invite* them to bring such questions to you in the future, indicating there are truths of our faith that speak directly to these questions.

RESPONDING TO ASSUMPTIONS ABOUT A CHILD'S SEXUAL ORIENTATION

Elias, a new second grader, just finished his first day of school. When you ask him how his day was, he starts to cry. After giving him a long hug, you ask him to tell you what happened. Elias says, "This boy called me gay. What does 'gay' mean? Am I gay?" Keep in mind that Elias is seven years old.

This is a teachable moment for Elias, and it can help you have conversations about sexuality in the future, regardless of his eventual patterns of attraction. You may be feeling a lot of things in this moment: angry, protective, anxious, and so much more.

How could you respond? Here's one way:

> "I am sorry that happened. How confusing. It sounds like those boys were being mean. 'Gay' is a word that older people may use to talk about someone's attraction, like who a person has a crush on. Most people are attracted to the opposite sex. For example, I am attracted to your dad, and I am a woman and he is a man. Some women find themselves attracted to other women and some men find themselves attracted to other men. Attraction doesn't usually show up for several more years. You don't have to worry about that now. No matter who you are attracted to someday, you can tell your parents. God has a beautiful plan for your life, and you are his beloved child.[20] He wants you to become a saint and will help you no matter what comes! And no kids get to tell you what words to use to talk about yourself. When a kid is being mean, or is bringing something up in a group that is not for them to talk about, you can always tell them to stop and tell a teacher. You can also ignore them."

HOW DO WE RESPOND TO PORTRAYALS OF LGBTQ-IDENTIFIED PEOPLE IN MEDIA?

Many young Christians I meet with who are sexual minorities or gender minorities have struggled to find other Christians "like them." Especially when they feel compelled to follow a Christian sexual ethic, they often feel caught between two worlds: the mainstream LGBTQ community and the Church. They might look to LGBTQ-identified people in media to understand their experience, even if media doesn't always offer role models who have similar Christian values.

Many Christian parents, on the other hand, get worried about their children having access to media portrayals of LGBTQ experiences. Often, they block their children from seeing these portrayals, pretend they don't exist, or never discuss them. This leaves young people fending for themselves in trying to engage with media maturely and reflectively.

I think of Kendall, a sixteen-year-old who shared with me in therapy about what her faith community and her family thinks about her attraction to women. Kendall said, "They would never accept me. They would be disgusted by me if they knew." Despite her commitment to chastity and her own willingness to forego a same-sex relationship because of her beliefs about marriage, she was terrified to tell anyone about her attractions.

I never want to assume whether or not a family would be receptive to this disclosure, so I asked Kendall how she had concluded that she couldn't tell anyone. She said, "You should hear how they respond when the topic of gay or transgender people comes up. Whether it's in a commercial, in a TV show, on the news, or at the dinner table, the look on my dad's face says it all." His look, she explained, was a look of disgust and disdain. Because he reacted poorly to LGBTQ-identifying people portrayed in media, Kendall felt sure he would react poorly to her as well.

This type of story is heartbreaking to me for many reasons, and it illustrates a really important point: Your kids are watching you. When you respond in disgust or hatred to an LGBTQ-identifying person, that will impact your child's perspective about how you care for people. More than that, it will impact whether your child believes your words when you later say something like, "We love everyone and respect everyone, even people we may disagree with." Our actions speak louder than our words in these moments.

Moreover, when young kids observe this behavior and then later become aware of their own same-sex sexuality within a family culture that sends this messaging, it's going to be nearly impossible at first for them to believe any words said by parents that reflect their belovedness. Instead, they will internalize things like, "I am disgusting," or "I am bad," without anyone ever knowing it's happening. The long-term impacts of such messaging are hard to fully appreciate and may be one reason why so many young people walk away from faith when they experience same-sex sexuality or gender dysphoria.

Many Christians grieve the fact that we are portrayed in media as bigoted and prejudiced against sexual and gender minorities because of our beliefs about things like marriage and sexual ethics. Unfortunately, the criticism against us is not completely unfounded. How many of you reading have witnessed a Christian speak harshly and mockingly about LGBTQ-identifying person? I know I have. The way we respond matters. If we say nothing, that also matters. The adage holds true: actions speak louder than words.

Now that we've outlined what not to do (displays of disgust, hostility, and shaming) and why (because it impacts children's beliefs about others, and in some cases about themselves), I also want to discuss how to engage with children about media.

Let's make it practical. Say a makeup advertisement with Jazz Jennings comes on as your family is watching a sporting event.[21] Jazz is a prominent transgender young person in the United States who has her own reality show. Imagine your child, age five, says, "In my kindergarten class, my friend said Jazz is a boy who became a girl. What does that mean?"

This is where a distinction between "position" and "posture" is really helpful.[22] Position involves our Catholic beliefs, grounded in natural law, natural sciences, and an understanding of the reality of objective truth as it relates to matters such as human sexuality. Posture involves our actual way of relating to real people, including those who reject a Catholic understanding of human sexuality. Posture flows out of and incorporates our position, and at the same time our posture draws from discernment of how to prudently respond in particular moments and conversations.

How could you use the position-versus-posture distinction in the case of the Jazz commercial?

Here's one way you could approach the conversation:

"I am so glad you told me about what happened in class. It's so nice we can talk about these things. What did you think of what your friend said?"

After the child shares their reaction, you could say something like this to help them understand your position (adapted to your own Christian convictions):

> "As Catholics, we believe that our bodies matter and are reflective of our souls. God had a plan when he created someone as a boy or a girl, and you can't just simply become a boy if you are born a girl or become a girl if you are born a boy. Our being born as a boy or as a girl isn't random. Your body is a gift and can do so many wonderful things as it is."

Then help your child understand how that position relates to your posture:

> "People like Jazz exist and their lives matter. There are people who were born a boy and have lots of pain about that or were born a girl and have lots of pain about that. Again, it's not as easy as becoming a different gender, but we know that God loves Jazz, and we can treat people like Jazz with care and respect. We can also, when we know someone who struggles in this way, help them find ways to serve God and grow in understanding of his plan for them."

DISCUSSING SAME-SEX MARRIAGE

The same application of position and posture can be helpful when talking about same-sex sexuality. Let's imagine your child, Cody, goes to school and has a friend who has two parents who are both women. Cody asks one day after school, "Why does my friend Joey have two moms, and I have a mom and a dad?"

Here's an answer you could give that addresses both position and posture:

> "Good question, Cody! You know how Mom and Dad are married? Some kids have different situations than that. Your cousin Cassie lives with her mom but not her dad. And Joey has two moms, and we don't know about Joey's dad. Our position is that

> God's plan for marriage is that it's between a man and a woman. Some people don't live according to that plan, and we believe that other types of relationship aren't the same as Christian marriage. Our posture is that we see every person, including Joey and his moms, as people we are called to treat with respect and value as people. I am sure Joey loves his moms, and so we don't want to act as if Joey is lacking because he doesn't have a dad. I am grateful that you get to know Joey and want to learn more about him and his family. As we grow up, we get the chance to share our beliefs with others to help them explore more of God's plan for their life, and that is something that takes prayer and talking with God about when and how to communicate those truths."

The tone you use when talking about sexual minorities is really important, especially since some of our Christian young people will grow up to experience attraction to the same sex, and many more will have family and friends who identify as LGBTQ. The way you respond to your child's questions will model for them how Christians are called to treat people who experience same-sex sexuality. I encourage you to lead with compassion, acknowledging that gay people exist, that they're in our churches and communities, and that God has a good plan for the lives of sexual minorities, which is revealed gradually in the context of a real relationship with God and the Body of Christ.

As we wrap up this chapter, I recognize that many more questions will arise as you engage with your child about sexuality and gender in real time. This chapter can't account for every moment—it would take a whole book, and much more, to address such complex issues in detail. But my hope is that this chapter gives you a starting point to respond to your young child's questions more effectively than you previously could. I hope it also equips you to create space in your home for active and ongoing conversations about sexuality and gender long before puberty. It is never too early to show your kids that you want to know what they are thinking about, as it relates to sexual and gender minority experiences as much as anything else.

CHAPTER 10

"HOW DO I NAVIGATE TECHNOLOGY ACCESS?"

SETTING YOUR CHILD UP FOR SUCCESS IN A DIGITAL AGE

In this chapter, we'll discuss your child's access to technology more broadly and to pornographic content specifically. I want to help you begin preparing your kids for the challenges they will face in today's digital world.

We'll begin with some practical advice to help adults monitor and shape kids' access to social media. Some of this advice will address general media use, but most of it will focus on avoiding dangerous situations that can come through technology use. Next, I want to highlight how early exposure to sexual content—which is now more likely than ever to come through television, computers, or phone-based apps—can impact sexual development. Finally, I'll begin a conversation that will continue in book 2 about how we respond after we become aware that a young person is viewing pornography.

INITIAL CONSIDERATIONS ABOUT TECHNOLOGY AND SOCIAL MEDIA

I have a love-hate relationship with social media. I won't tell you that it's all bad, because that would be extremely hypocritical, and I don't truly believe it. From both a research perspective and a clinical perspective, I have seen the value of social media in real time. Apps have helped some of my clients gain the necessary support, accountability, and connections to stop harmful behaviors, including cutting. During a global pandemic in 2020, social media allowed people to maintain lifesaving connections and bonds—in some cases, literally *lifesaving*. There are times on hard days when a video on social media can make a room of people erupt in much-needed laughter.

Yet I've also seen the downside of social media, as I'm sure you also have. Cyberbullying and all forms of online cruelty, whether by children or by adults, can take an enormous toll over time. Extended technology use by people who are already lonely can actually increase their feelings of loneliness.[1] And many teen and adult clients, when they take even an hour-long daily "pause" from social media, report feeling less anxious, more refreshed, and more motivated. Perhaps most distressingly, technological advances—specifically through social media—have made pornographic content easier than ever to access from anywhere and at any time, thereby increasing the global demand for pornography.

Social media, like all technology, is a tool, and one that can be used well or poorly by any one of us. Since it is a tool, we need to learn the "user manual" attached to it. This is how we can learn to use it properly rather than harmfully. If we are unable to use it properly, we are better off not using it at all.

BOUNDARIES AROUND ACCESS

Because technology is a powerful tool, it's fitting for us to set boundaries around the ways we access and use technology, just as we would for any other powerful tool. We can divide this conversation about boundaries into four questions: "Who?" "What?" "Where and when?" "Why?"

WHO?

The first question about technology access is quite simple: Who is allowed to access it, and with whom is access allowed?

For any child, especially if they're under ten, parental supervision is critical. One of the biggest challenges with providing adequate supervision is that more kids than ever use phones or tablets.[2] Gone are the days of a family computer or a single television. This makes monitoring all the more important and all the more difficult. If you can't monitor the device, I wouldn't advise giving it to your child.

RECOMMENDED SCREEN TIME LIMITS[3]

Age	Recommended Screen Time
0–18 months	Limit to video chatting with out-of-town family/friends, always with an adult sitting with child. Whenever possible, do not have television on in the background.
18–24 months	Limit to watching educational programs, always with an adult present to discuss and engage content.
2–5 years old	Limit noneducational programming to 1 hour on weekdays and 3 hours on weekend days, with an adult present in the room whenever possible.
6 and up	Limit activities that include screens to promote healthy activities.

WHAT?

Next, what exactly is allowed? It's worth picking one or several options that you feel are age-appropriate for your kids. A good rule of thumb is to make sure you've watched at least one episode of any show along with your kids before allowing them to watch the rest. If you haven't been able to watch a show and get a sense for it, then it's probably best not to let it be an option for your kids. This helps you understand the media your child is consuming so you can process it with them and vet potentially unhelpful media.

This might mean creating a list of shows or movies that you think would be helpful for your child at various ages. Remember to tell other people your child spends time with the list of shows they're allowed to watch, so that your kids don't accidentally end up watching things they aren't ready for.

When kids crave screens, see if you can find audiobooks and music for them to listen to that don't involve a visual component. This is a good transition activity if a child is being weaned off screen time and having difficulty with it. As always, give options: "We are going to stop screen time for today. We can either listen to nothing and be quiet for a bit, or we can listen to a song. Which would you like? Nothing or a song?" Giving options is a way to get out of a power struggle, while making sure only to give options that you approve of.

WHERE AND WHEN?

It's worth identifying space and places that you will allow screens and those you won't. Establishing this family rule early on will help your children identify places where, as they get older, it is more acceptable to use a phone. It also builds a foundation of skills for managing and limiting technology access and use in the years to come.

- Appropriate Settings: couch in living area, car seat (during car rides)
- Inappropriate Settings: meals or dinner table, bedroom, alone, during family or social activities, while doing homework

I've already suggested appropriate lengths of time to watch screens by age group. But it's also important to know what times of day screens should be avoided. A good rule of thumb is to have no screens an hour before bedtime. Screens stimulate our brain to wake up, which will make it harder to calm down and prepare for sleep.

WHY?

This is where you get to have conversations with your kid. They may want to know why friends can watch screens "whenever they want," while your family has stricter rules. You can have conversations with your kids early and often about what screens are for and what they are not for:

"You like screens, don't you! What do you like about them? You like to watch your shows and listen to music. Me too! Screens are one way to have fun, but not the only way. To grow, we need to have fun in lots of different ways! When we are bored, screens are not the best way to have fun. Let's pick something else to do now."

CONSEQUENCES OF TOO MUCH SCREEN TIME[4]

- Difficulties with sleep
- Poor grades in school
- Reading fewer books
- Spending less time socializing
- Staying inside more and doing less physical activity
- Mood changes
- Negative self-image and body-image comments or concerns
- Obsession over what other peers are doing and strong tendency to compare
- Difficulty finding alternative ways to unwind and entertain

If you aren't modeling appropriate screen time, it will be much more difficult to implement boundaries for your kids. So if you struggle yourself with putting the screen down, start there. It will help more than you realize!

INTERNET SAFETY

Internet safety, like any other type of safety, is important to teach before a child has access to the internet. You would not let your child bake cookies alone if they didn't know that metal gets hot. In the same way, don't let your child get on the internet without making sure they understand the dangers therein.

There are increasingly available resources for establishing and maintaining internet safety.[5] We will revisit the conversation on resources in book 2 of this series. For now, I want to offer an Internet Access Plan that you can use to teach your elementary-school kids about internet safety.

This will help you and your kids feel more able to protect against any threats that could come your way.

INTERNET ACCESS PLAN

- I will write my passwords down in a private place that my parents can access. I will share them with no one else. Other than me, only my parents can know my passwords.
- I will be kind to anyone and everyone I encounter online.
- Online friends are not the same as in-person friends. It takes more time to build trust with people I meet online. I will only add friends online with my parents' permission.
- I will disable chats in online games. If I gain access to chats, I will not chat with a person unless my parent(s) and I have met them in person.
- There are bad people who try to hurt kids they meet online. I will not talk to strangers or agree to meet with strangers, no matter how nice they seem.
- I will only use phones and computers in open spaces of my home.
- If people ask details about my life, I will use a fake name and will never give my address, send photos, tell my birthdate, or give any other identifying information.

EXPOSURE TO PORNOGRAPHY

It is heartbreaking to have to write about pornography in a book about parenting children below the age of ten. Unfortunately, as you may already know, the average age of first exposure to pornography is around eleven.[7] Additionally, one in twenty-five primary-school kids have already been sent a naked or semi-naked picture by an adult.[8] This risk of exposure to porn demands even earlier preemptive conversation with a child than ever before.

When I talk to adults who can't stop watching porn, I'm struck that many of them first saw pornography by happenstance. They didn't seek it out. It seemed to seek them out. Pornography exposure can happen through friends at a sleepover or playdate, through an app or social media popup, in a "stash" of a parent's pornography through bookmarked internet pages, in magazines, or when opening someone else's computer or smartphone.

Early exposure to pornography can be traumatizing for a young child. While the word "traumatic" is often overused, I mean it here in the literal sense. Pornography exposure often exceeds a child's capacity to cope and violates them in a profound way. It evokes many of the same emotions as sexual abuse, including powerlessness, helplessness, confusion, and shame. The impacts of this exposure are significant and hard to predict.

I have walked with clients who, through early exposure to pornography, began having intrusive sexual thoughts that later manifested in obsessive compulsive disorder. For many years, they could not figure out why they couldn't get distressing content out of their heads. It seemed to be their brain's way of saying, "Something intruded when you were young," and their brain was right. Facing this reality was essential for their healing. It helped reduce the pain of their intrusive thoughts and gave them enough space to acknowledge the early experiences that had set a trajectory for their life without their permission or consent.

While children will develop into adult sexual beings, sexuality is not typically in the forefront of their minds in early childhood, nor need it be! Remember, when a child gets overly focused on sexual content, it is a warning sign of sexual abuse or other kinds of abuse or neglect. It is not developmentally normal for young children to think about one another and themselves in sexualized ways. This is one of the precious things about childhood.

A close friend recounted to me recently how terrified she is of her young children one day watching pornography. Fortunately, there are ways to prepare for and anticipate future exposure to pornography, even as you hope these moments never come.

As your child is around other children who are also likely exposed to or talking about sexual content, you could hint at the possibility that they might encounter this kind of content. Try making it less about individual playmates a child is spending time with and more general. For example, you could say this:

> "As you get a bit older, you get to have more time with your friends. Just like we have talked about before, we have house rules that apply even when we aren't in our home. Can you remember one? [Try to get your child talking. Maybe they will reference no mandatory hugs, no touching of one another's genitals, etc.] That's right! Another rule is that we do not view pictures or videos of naked people, whether they're strangers or people we know. Those things are private. Believe it or not, sometimes people try to show other people those things. They can pop up on a computer or phone, or a friend can show them. If someone ever showed you something like that, what could you do?"

After your child answers, you could help them generate additional ideas of how to respond:

- Turn your face away and look away.
- Walk away.
- Close your eyes.
- Ask them to stop.
- Point out how strange it is to look at pictures of people we don't know.
- Say, "That's private!"
- Tell a trusted adult (including a parent).

WHEN THEY HAVE SEEN PORNOGRAPHY

Let's say that you've found your eight-year-old looking at a video on your phone with a naked body. What is a helpful way to respond?

As I've emphasized throughout this book, stay as calm as you can. It's better to not respond at all in the moment than to react out of your own panic, anger, or whatever else might come up. Pause. Check in with yourself. Ask yourself what you are feeling. Remind yourself that this is not an emergency. If you need time before you speak to what happened, give yourself that time. Then come back when you are ready to talk calmly. A calm tone will go further than you know in signaling that you are ready to face this (even if inside you don't feel ready)!

1) Begin by telling your child that you are grateful you saw what they were watching, so that you can talk about it: "I am so grateful I came across that, so we can talk about it."

2) Reflect what you saw: "I noticed there were some pictures/videos of naked bodies of strangers on the phone when you were holding it."

3) Ask open-ended questions: "How did those come up?" Remember, it is actually much more likely at this age that the pornographic images popped up than it is that your child sought them out. If a child says the images "just came up," you are better off believing them than going into detective mode. You can acknowledge, "That can happen." It also helps to clarify, "Whether you looked it up or it popped up, I would not be mad at you. I am asking to understand what happened."

Regardless of how the images appeared, invite your child to reflect on their experience: "What did you think of what you saw? What did you feel when you saw it?"

Validate the feelings that come up. Kids can feel lots of things: shocked, curious, scared, disgusted, confused, embarrassed, pleasurable.

4) Normalize their curiosity to reduce shame:

> "It is normal to be curious about people's bodies. But those types of videos of strangers are not helpful ways to learn about our bodies. Remember, our naked bodies are a gift from God. Our bodies are private. They aren't meant for strangers to see. Strangers' bodies aren't meant for us to see. Some people don't know that, but we know that. So, when we see naked bodies, as beautiful and good as they are, we can look away or close our eyes to give them respect."

5) Plan for next time:

> "Sometimes friends will try to show us pictures or videos of naked bodies. Or things can pop up online like we just saw on the phone. When that happens, just like today, I want to know so I can help you with that. So, if that happens on the phone again, I can help. And if friends or strangers ever show you things like that, remember that bodies are good and not to be seen by just anybody. So, you can always say

no. If someone doesn't listen when you say no, look away, even if you are curious. And as always, we can talk about it after. Okay? Any questions?"

GIRLS AND PORNOGRAPHY EXPOSURE

Pornography exposure is not solely a problem for young boys. Too often, people assume that if I am talking about clients who are dealing with habitual porn use, those people are men. This assumption translates into their conversations with their children. Parents are often less likely to consider that their daughters, like their sons, have access to technology that will expose them to porn sooner and sooner all the time. And our girls, like our boys, can get hooked.

I remember one Catholic young woman I was working with who shared with me about her ongoing porn use. She explained that when she first began viewing porn, "I didn't even know that what I was doing when I was watching it was masturbating, because I only ever heard about masturbation in youth group as something boys did. Everyone assumed girls didn't, so I didn't put two and two together until I got to college and heard girls talking about it. But it was confusing, because my girlfriends told me nothing was wrong with it. That just made me more confused than ever."

This is yet another reason why it's so important to talk with kids about their bodies and sexuality early and often. How different that client's life could have been if trusted adults had taught her that pornography and masturbation do not discriminate between the sexes. She needed to hear that she was not alone in her compulsion toward pornography, and that there were ways to address her habit over time with the help of others.

None of us can manage life alone, and that's as true for exposure to pornography as anything else. The good news is, with your help, your kids don't have to face any of this challenging territory alone!

EPILOGUE

As I write this epilogue, my heart is swelling with gratitude for each of you who has taken the time to read this book. This beautiful, hard, and sanctifying life is better with each of us seeking to make the world safer for our children. It is no small thing to prioritize the well-being of the next generation. My hope is that you will glimpse the fruits of your labors in this life, and all the more in the life to come.

If even one child is safeguarded from abuse because of your reading this book, it will be worth it. But of course, we don't just do this work to keep our children away from bad things. We also do it, far more importantly, to make way for all that is good.

I pray that our children can clearly see the dignity of their bodies and can surround themselves with those who mirror this dignity. I pray that our children can take hold of a Christian sexual ethic with conviction and gratitude for the safeguards it offers. I pray that our children can grow into healthy and holy adults who glorify God in and through their sexuality, regardless of their vocation in life. With God's grace, and a little bit of education, I pray that we can cultivate families, churches, and schools where this prayer is realized.

APPENDIX

RESOURCES REGARDING MENTAL HEALTH AND COPING

BOOKS ON MINDFULNESS

Gregory Bottaro, *The Mindful Catholic: Finding God One Moment at a Time.*

BOOKS ON TEACHING COPING TO KIDS

Gregory and Barbra Bottaro, *Sitting Like a Saint: Catholic Mindfulness for Kids.*

Daniel Siegel and Tina Payne Bryson, *The Whole-Brain Child: 12 Revolutionary Strategies to Nurture Your Child's Developing Mind.*

RESOURCES REGARDING GENDER

Mark Yarhouse, *Understanding Gender Dysphoria.*

Mark Yarhouse and Julia Sadusky, *Emerging Gender Identities: Understanding the Diverse Experiences of Today's Youth.*

Mark Yarhouse and Julia Sadusky, *Gender Identity and Faith: Clinical Postures, Tools, and Case Studies for Client-Centered Care.*

Abigail Favale, *The Genesis of Gender.*

RESOURCES REGARDING SAME-SEX SEXUALITY

ORGANIZATIONS

Eden Invitation
Revoice
Kaleidoscope
EQUIP
Center for Faith, Sexuality and Gender
Posture Shift

BOOKS

Eve Tushnet, *Gay and Catholic; Tenderness.*

Greg Coles, *Single, Gay and Christian; No Longer Strangers.*

Greg Johnson, *Still Time to Care: What We Can Learn from the Church's Failed Attempt to Cure Homosexuality.*

Matt and Laurie Krieg, *An Impossible Marriage.*

Caleb Kaltenbach, *Messy Grace; Messy Truth.*

Mark Yarhouse and Olya Zaporozhets, *Costly Obedience.*

Mark Yarhouse, *Understanding Sexual Identity.*

Mark Yarhouse, Janet Dean, Michael Lastoria, and Stephen Stratton, *Listening to Sexual Minorities.*

PODCASTS

Life on Side B

RESOURCES REGARDING SEXUAL TRAUMA AND PROCESSING

BOOKS

Bessel van der Kolk, *The Body Keeps the Score: Brain, Mind, and Body in the Healing of Trauma.*

Pete Walker, *Complex PTSD: From Surviving to Thriving.*

Lindsay C. Gibson, *Adult Children of Emotionally Immature Parents: How to Heal from Distant, Rejecting, or Self-Involved Parents; Recovering from Emotionally Immature Parents: Practical Tools to Establish Boundaries and Reclaim Your Emotional Autonomy.*

Mark Wolynn, *It Didn't Start with You: How Inherited Family Trauma Shapes Who We Are and How to End the Cycle.*

Richard Schwartz, *No Bad Parts: Healing Trauma and Restoring Wholeness with the Internal Family Systems Model*

PODCASTS

The Place We Find Ourselves

Matthias J. Barker Podcast

RESOURCES REGARDING SHAME AND VULNERABILITY

Curt Thompson, *The Soul of Shame.*

Brené Brown, *The Power of Vulnerability: Teachings of Authenticity, Connection, and Courage; The Gifts of Imperfection.*

RESOURCES REGARDING PORNOGRAPHY / SEXUAL SELF-HATRED / COMPULSIVE SEXUAL BEHAVIORS

BOOKS

Jay Stringer, *Unwanted: How Sexual Brokenness Reveals Our Way to Healing.*

Patrick Carnes, *Out of the Shadows; Facing the Shadow; Sexual Anorexia; In the Shadows of the Net; Contrary to Love: Helping the Sexual Addict.*

Books for Women Specifically

Marnie Ferree, *No Stones: Women Redeemed from Sexual Addiction.*

RESOURCES REGARDING PROTECTING CHILDREN FROM INAPPROPRIATE ONLINE CONTENT

Common Sense Media

Child Rescue Coalition

RESOURCES REGARDING TALKING WITH YOUR CHILD ABOUT SEXUALITY

Birds & Bees Online Course

GivingtheTalk.com

NOTES

INTRODUCTION

1. Jay Stringer, *Unwanted: How Sexual Brokenness Reveals Our Way to Healing* (Carol Stream, IL: NavPress, 2018), 31–44.

1. "WHY AM I HAVING SUCH A HARD TIME STARTING THE CONVERSATION?"

1. Pope St. John Paul II's collection of talks about human sexuality have been brought together in book form in *Man and Woman He Created Them: A Theology of the Body* (St. Louis: Pauline Books & Media, 2006).

2. Pope Francis reflects on this in *Amoris Laetitia,* where he notes that "begetting and raising children, for its part, mirrors God's creative work." See *Amoris Laetitia of the Holy Father Francis to Bishops, Priests, and Deacons, Consecrated Persons, Christian Married Couples and All the Lay Faithful,* March 19, 2016, no. 29, www.vatican.va/content/dam/francesco/pdf/apost_exhortations/documents/papa-francesco_esortazione-ap_20160319_amoris-laetitia_en.pdf.

3. *Catechism of the Catholic Church,* 2nd ed. (Washington, DC: United States Catholic Conference, 2000), no. 260.

4. *Catechism,* nos. 645–48.

5. *Catechism,* no. 1701.

6. See Genesis 3:7–10.

7. "Child Sexual Abuse Statistics," Darkness to Light, n.d., accessed March 15, 2023, www.d2l.org/wp-content/uploads/2017/01/all_statistics_20150619.pdf.

8. Howard N. Snyder, "Sexual Assault of Young Children as Reported to Law Enforcement: Victim, Incident and Offender Characteristics," *Bureau of Justice Statistics*, July 2000, 1–14, https://bjs.ojp.gov/content/pub/pdf/saycrle.pdf.

9. "Child Sexual Abuse Statistics."

10. "Child Sexual Abuse Statistics."

2. "WHAT IS THIS?"

1. This information is adapted from a helpful *Healthline* article outlining the parts and function of male genitalia. Jill Seladi-Schulman, "Everything to Know about Male Genitalia," *Healthline*, June 5, 2020, accessed October 8, 2022, www.healthline.com/health/mens-health/male-genitalia.

2. This information is adapted from an article about the external female genital organs. Jessica E. McLaughlin, "Female External Genital Organs," *Merck Manual Consumer Version*, last modified September 2022, www.merckmanuals.com/home/women-s-health-issues/biology-of-the-female-reproductive-system/female-external-genital-organs.

3. The information is adapted from an article about the internal female organs. Jessica E. McLaughlin, "Female Internal Genital Organs," *Merck Manual Consumer Version*, last modified September 2022, www.merckmanuals.com/home/women-s-health-issues/biology-of-the-female-reproductive-system/female-internal-genital-organs.

4. Kristine Ives, "Actual Anatomy: Teaching Your Children Body Parts," Colorado Coalition Against Sexual Assault, July 21, 2015, www.ccasa.org/actual-anatomy-teaching-your-children-body-parts/. "Teaching children anatomically correct terms, age-appropriately," says Laura Palumbo, a prevention specialist with the National Sexual Violence Resource Center (NSVRC), "promotes positive body image, self-confidence, and parent-child communication; discourages perpetrators; and,

in the event of abuse, helps children and adults navigate the disclosure and forensic interview process" (ibid).

3. "WHAT IS HEALTHY EXPLORATION?"

1. "Privacy," Oxford Dictionary of English, 3rd ed., accessed October 2, 2022, www.oxfordlearnersdictionaries.com/definition/english/privacy.

2. "Privacy."

3. "What Is Age-Appropriate Sexual Curiosity?," *Bark* blog, December 6, 2020, www.bark.us/blog/appropriate-age-sexual-curiosity/.

4. "Sexual Behaviors in Young Children: What's Normal, What's Not?" American Academy of Pediatrics, HealthyChildren.org, April 1, 2019, www.healthychildren.org/English/ages-stages/preschool/Pages/Sexual-Behaviors-Young-Children.aspx.

5. Nancy D. Kellogg, "Clinical Report—The Evaluation of Sexual Behaviors in Children," American Academy of Pediatrics, 2009, www.icmec.org/wp-content/uploads/2017/04/AAP-evaluation-of-sexual-behavior-in-children.pdf.

4. "SHOULD I MAKE THEM HUG STRANGERS?"

1. This comes out of feedback provided by Chris Damian regarding the way in which different cultural groups may have embedded norms around physical affections that depict a sign of respect. He rightly highlighted that some of what I have written here will bump up against certain cultural norms and values in such a way that more dialogue is warranted.

2. A resource that can be very helpful for learning how to set boundaries is Henry Cloud, *Boundaries, Updated and Expanded Edition: When to Say Yes, How to Say No to Take Control of Your Life* (Grand Rapids, MI: Zondervan, 2017).

5. "HOW DO THEY LEARN TO SAY NO?"

1. "Sexual Development and Behavior in Children: Information for Parents and Caregivers," National Child Traumatic Stress Network, April 2009, page 3, www.nctsn.org/sites/default/files/resources/sexual_development_and_behavior_in_children.pdf.

2. Christine Emba, "Consent Is Not Enough. We Need a New Sexual Ethic," *Washington Post*, March 17, 2022, www.washingtonpost.com/opinions/2022/03/17/sex-ethics-rethinking-consent-culture/.

7. "WHAT DO I DO IF THEY TELL ME SOMETHING BAD HAPPENED TO THEM?"

1. Find additional resources on childhood sexual abuse here, including common warning signs that can help you identify child abuse more quickly. "Keeping Kids Safe: Warning Signs of Child Sexual Abuse," Michigan State University, accessed March 22, 2023, www.canr.msu.edu/creating-safe-environments/uploads/files/Warning%20Signs%20of%20Child%20Sexual%20Abuse%20Final.pdf.

8. "WHAT DO I DO ABOUT SLEEPOVERS OR OVERNIGHT TRIPS?"

1. One of the most helpful accounts I follow on social media related to child safety is the Child Rescue Coalition. They are on the front lines of protecting children who have been sexually abused, especially by developing technology to identify predators of children. They offer a list of incredibly helpful tips when it comes to preparing for sleepovers, when those occur. I have incorporated some of their suggestions within the breakout box. Child Rescue Coalition, accessed September 23, 2022, https://childrescuecoalition.org/.

2. Birds & Bees is an online course that provides information for talking about sexuality with your kids. In their course and on their Instagram page, they also recommend using "seed" instead of sperm with younger children. They offer helpful examples of how to talk about the sperm as a "seed" and hint at other creatures that come from seeds and eggs to illustrate this in familiar terms for a child. For example, a way you could say this is: "Trees grow from seeds and so do humans. The type of seeds that humans come from are sperm." Birds & Bees, "The Course," accessed March 22, 2023, https://birds-bees.com/pages/courses.

3. Álvaro López Soto et al., "Sonographic Measure Techniques of Fetal Penile Length," *Obstetrics & Gynecology Science* 63, no. 5 (September 2020): 555–64, www.ncbi.nlm.nih.gov/pmc/articles/PMC7494763/.

4. Erections do not lead to ejaculation in early childhood, because sperm are not present in a boy's testicles until puberty.

5. Susan Taylor, "Everything You Wanted to Know about Little Boys and Their Erections," Babyology, September 4, 2018, babyology.com.au/health/family-health/awkward-everything-to-know-about-little-boys-and-their-erections/.

9. "HOW DO I TALK WITH MY CHILD ABOUT GENDER AND SAME-SEX SEXUALITY?"

1. I have coauthored two books on the topic of gender. One, *Emerging Gender Identities: Understanding the Diverse Experiences of Today's Youth,* is written for those seeking to understand the changing landscape around gender and how to accompany youth who are exploring gender and/or experiencing gender-related distress. The other, *Gender Identity & Faith: Clinical Postures, Tools, and Case Studies for Client-Centered Care,* is for mental-health professionals looking to accompany people of faith who are exploring gender in therapy.

2. Pope Francis has addressed gender theory in multiple places, with some notable attention given in his papal encyclical *Amoris Laetitia*. See *Amoris Laetitia of the Holy Father Francis to Bishops, Priests, and Deacons, Consecrated Persons, Christian Married Couples and All the Lay Faithful,* March 19, 2016, no. 56, www.vatican.va/content/dam/francesco/pdf/apost_exhortations/documents/papa-francesco_esortazione-ap_20160319_amoris-laetitia_en.pdf.

3. Abigail Favale coined the phrase "gender paradigm" in her book *The Genesis of Gender* to offer a nimbler way of engaging with perspectives on gender that focus on gender as a social construct that people "perform" rather than an essential and objective aspect of the human experience. The idea of gender as performative comes from the writings of Judith Butler in *Gender Trouble*. Abigail Favale, *The Genesis of Gender* (San Francisco: Ignatius Press, 2022), 30.

4. There is a debate in Christian circles around the appropriateness of various terms to describe people who experience sexual attraction to people of the same sex. Some people prefer the term "same-sex attraction/attracted," others prefer "same-sex desire," and still others prefer "gay/lesbian/bisexual." When I use "same-sex sexuality," I am attempting to

use an intentionally descriptive and broad term that accounts for a range of people who use a range of labels, all of whom experience the commonality of sexual attraction to the same sex, without relying on labels that are subject to significant debate. I do not use the term "same-sex sexuality" to imply that a person's sexuality is reducible to their patterns of attraction, but rather that one's pattern of sexual desires relate to and impact the experience of sexuality in a meaningful way for each person, with sexual minorities being no exception. Sexuality, according to the *Catechism of the Catholic Church*, is more broadly said to incorporate "all aspects of the human person in the unity of his body and soul. It especially concerns affectivity, the capacity to love and to procreate, and in a more general way the aptitude for forming bonds of communion with others." Thus sexuality, within a Catholic understanding, can include a person's sexual desires as a human person and affectivity, among other factors. See *Catechism of the Catholic Church*, 2nd ed. (Washington, DC: United States Catholic Conference, 2000), no. 2332.

5. *Catechism of the Catholic Church*, 2nd ed. (Washington, DC: United States Catholic Conference, 2000), no. 2358.

6. While I am aware of times where a parent may decide to set firm boundaries with an LGBTQ-identified person because that person has repeatedly undermined the parents' efforts to teach a Catholic ethic or overtly villainized those who uphold that ethic in front of children, I more often see a fear-based approach that reactively cuts off contact with an LGBTQ-identified person without giving them opportunities to demonstrate maturity and respect of the family's values.

7. This finding comes from research available in *Listening to Sexual Minorities*, which is a book that presents longitudinal research on Christian sexual minorities on college campuses, and the milestone events related to first awareness of attractions and first disclosure of this to others, specifically family. Mark A. Yarhouse et al., *Listening to Sexual Minorities: A Study of Faith and Sexual Identity on Christian College Campuses* (Westmont, IL: InterVarsity Press, 2018), 66.

8. The framing of sexual stewardship is attributable to the writing and private conversations I have had with Mark Yarhouse. He first introduced this concept to me as another area of stewardship Christians are invited into by God, much in the same way that we are invited to have

stewardship over money, time, and talents. This offers a more positive framing around the goal of formation around sexual ethics and moves it away from more negative frames that focus on "what not to do."

9. This information is adapted from Caitlin Ryan's research out of the Family Acceptance Project. She found that avoiding what she called "rejecting behaviors" will protect a child from worsening depression and suicide. Caitlin Ryan et al., "Family Rejection as a Predictor of Negative Health Outcomes in White and Latino Lesbian, Gay, and Bisexual Young Adults," *Pediatrics* 123, no. 1 (January 2009): 346–52, https://pubmed.ncbi.nlm.nih.gov/19117902/.

10. A more comprehensive list of key terms around gender can be found in Mark Yarhouse and Julia Sadusky, *Emerging Gender Identities: Understanding the Diverse Experiences of Today's Youth* (Brazos Press, 2020). I won't offer a thorough treatment of the topic in this chapter, but if you want to learn more, *Emerging Gender Identities* will offer a more rich engagement than space allows here. The terms listed in this breakout box are summarized from definitions provided in trainings by Mark Yarhouse and myself regularly on these topics. Adapted from Mark Yarhouse and Julia Sadusky, "Gender Identity and Faith," MyCounselor Training, August 26, 2022. They were also accounted for in Mark Yarhouse and Julia Sadusky, "The Complexities of Gender Identity: Toward a More Nuanced Approach to the Transgender Experience," in *Understanding Transgender Identities: Four Views*, ed. James K. Bielby and Paul R. Eddy (Grand Rapids: Baker Academic, 2019) 101–30.

11. Some Christians will reject the use of terms like "gender identity," putting them in quotations or replacing them with the term "sexual identity," which they intend to mean a person's sexed identity as male or female. Because this is not how the term "sexual identity" is used in common vernacular, I have defined "gender identity" for the sake of clarity to describe a person's experience of self as male or female or an alternative gender identity. The term "sexual identity" is used in Church documents to talk about our fundamental identity as men and women. This can make it confusing to discuss such terms in spaces where this language is used differently. Despite some resistance to applying a distinction of gender from biological sex in popular Catholic contexts, *Relatio Finalis* states that, "According to the Christian principle, soul and body, biological sex as well and the social-cultural role of the sex (gender), can

be distinguished, but not separated." Thus, when I discuss gender here, I am doing so with the intention of distinguishing but not separating it completely from biological sex. See Michael G. Campbell, *Relatio Finalis: Synod 15—Final Relatio of the Synod of Bishops to the Holy Father, Francis, A Working English Translation from the Original Italian* (October 24, 2015), no. 58, https://stmikes.utoronto.ca/wp-content/uploads/2015/12/Relatio-Finalis.pdf.

12. See www.sciencedirect.com/science/article/pii/B9780128035061000127.

13. When I use "sexual identity," I mean by that an adoption of labels such as "heterosexual," "same-sex attracted," "sexual minority," "homosexual," "gay," "lesbian," "bisexual," etc. to indicate an aspect of their identity. Some Christians have shared concerns about the moral implications of using terms such as "gay," "lesbian," and "bisexual" to describe their experience or others' experience of same-sex sexual desire. I do not recommend that Christians begin by positioning ourselves to prescribe language to sexual minorities among us. Rather, I first recommend we seek to understand what draws people to use a certain term and what they mean to indicate by it. This protects us from making assumptions about a person's reasons for using labels, since our assumptions are often incorrect or reductive of the fuller picture. I also do not find any official magisterium documents that indicate there is moral value or preferential treatment of a person using one word, such as same-sex attracted, over another, such as gay, to describe their pattern of sexual desires, despite that being assumed often in Catholic circles and some Catholic ministry groups. In the 1986 letter to bishops from the Congregation for the Doctrine of the Faith on the pastoral care of sexual minorities, the term used is "homosexual persons" and the moral concern lies in individual homosexual sexual acts. There is no indication that various labels used to connote attraction patterns are moral concerns, although there is clarity that authentic care does not 'consider the person solely as a "heterosexual" or a "homosexual" and insists that every person has a fundamental identity: the creature of God, and by grace, his child and heir to eternal life.' Just as the Congregation for the Doctrine of Faith letter uses "homosexual person" without meaning that the group they are referencing is reducible to their attraction pattern, it has been my experience that many people use terms such as "gay, lesbian, or bisexual

person," without meaning that they or the group they are referencing are "solely" a gay person or reducible to their attraction pattern. Thus, prescribing one term over another, as the term itself makes it less or more likely that a person will be reduced to their orientation, goes further than what Church teaching has offered us. There are certainly many people who are reductive in their view of self regardless of the terms they use to describe themselves, and many who are able to see themselves holistically who utilize a range of words to describe aspects of their experience. See Congregation for the Doctrine of the Faith, *Letter to the Bishops of the Catholic Church on the Pastoral Care of Homosexual Persons*, (October 1, 1986), no. 16, www.vatican.va/roman_curia/congregations/cfaith/documents/rc_con_cfaith_doc_19861001_homosexual-persons_en.html.

14. When Gallup asked 12,000 adults about personal identification, 86.3% reported being straight/heterosexual, 6.6% did not say, and 7.1% identified as LGBT. Among all US adults, 1% identify as lesbian, 1.5% identify as gay, and 4% identify as bisexual. Jeffrey M. Jones, "LGBT Identification in US Ticks Up to 7.1%," *Gallup*, February 17, 2022, https://news.gallup.com/poll/389792/lgbt-identification-ticks-up.aspx. Of note, when it comes to sexual attraction, the most recently published data from National Health Statistics found that, among 18–44-year-old adults, 6% of men and 17% of women reported attraction that was not exclusively heterosexual, meaning that they have experienced some level of same-sex attraction in their life. Casey E. Copen, Anjani Changra, and Isaedmaria Febo-Vasquez, "Sexual Behavior, Sexual Attraction, and Sexual Orientation Among Adults Aged 18–44 in the United States: Data from the 2011–2013 National Survey of Family Growth," *National Health Statistics Report*, no. 88 (January 7, 2016), www.cdc.gov/nchs/data/nhsr/nhsr088.pdf.

15. Pope Francis reflects on this in *Amoris Laetitia*, where he expressed concerns about gender theory. He stated, "'biological sex and the socio-cultural role of sex (gender) can be distinguished but not separated.'. . . It is one thing to be understanding of human weakness and the complexities of life, and another to accept ideologies that attempt to sunder what are inseparable aspects of reality." See *Amoris Laetitia of the Holy Father Francis to Bishops, Priests, and Deacons, Consecrated Persons, Christian Married Couples and All the Lay Faithful*, March 19, 2016, no. 56,

www.vatican.va/content/dam/francesco/pdf/apost_exhortations/documents/papa-francesco_esortazione-ap_20160319_amoris-laetitia_en.pdf.

16. A more robust treatment of this is available in a book by Mark Yarhouse, which will address parenting those wrestling with gender identity. It is titled *Talking to Kids about Gender Identity* and will be available through Bethany House, a division of Baker Publishing Group. At the time of writing this resource, it was not yet available in print.

17. The Center for Faith, Sexuality and Gender can offer referrals for Christian mental-health professionals who offer this approach. Additionally, Mark Yarhouse, PsyD, and I can offer referrals or our clinical services to families in this position. You can find my contact information at www.juliasadusky.com and Mark Yarhouse's at www.wheaton.edu/academics/school-of-psychology-counseling-and-family-therapy/sexual-and-gender-identity-institute/about/.

18. In *Gender Identity and Faith*, we discuss more about the approach of parenting your child, including offering what we call "scaffolding" and "gender patience." Mark A. Yarhouse and Julia A. Sadusky, *Gender Identity and Faith: Clinical Postures, Tools, and Case Studies, for Client-Centered Care* (Downers Grove, IL: InterVarsity Press Academic, 2022), 57–63.

19. Alida Bouris et al., "Effects of Victimization and Violence on Suicidal Ideation and Behaviors among Sexual Minority and Heterosexual Adolescents," *LGBT Health* 3, no. 2 (2016): 153–61, https://pubmed.ncbi.nlm.nih.gov/26789401/.

20. The *Catechism of the Catholic Church*, in addressing same-sex sexuality, describes sexual minorities as being capable of and called to self-mastery and the heights of Christian perfection. This presents a positive vision for the lives of Christians who experience same-sex sexuality. I want to equip you to provide this positive vision to your children, long before they move through puberty and become aware of their own sexual desires. This means not stopping at teaching about moral considerations around same-sex sexual behavior but also acknowledging and addressing the longing of each person for spaces to cultivate "inner freedom," through "disinterested friendship, by prayer and sacramental grace." If young people are not able to talk about their sexuality with their parents openly, cultivating virtue in this area becomes much more difficult. See

Catechism of the Catholic Church, 2nd ed. (Washington, DC: United States Catholic Conference, 2000), no. 2359.

21. Jazz Jennings is one of the youngest people to be identified as having gender dysphoria in the United States. Her family's story has been followed since she was very young, most notably in interviews with Barbara Walters when she was a child. She has since transitioned socially and medically.

22. This distinction comes out of language developed by Posture Shift and the work of Bill Henson. It was first explained to me by Meg Baatz, who articulated the distinction and how it can be helpful in these conversations.

10. "HOW DO I NAVIGATE TECHNOLOGY ACCESS?"

1. Melissa G. Hunt et al., "No More FOMO: Limiting Social Media Decreases Loneliness and Depression," *Journal of Social and Clinical Psychology* 37, no. 10 (December 2018): 751–68, https://doi.org/10.1521/jscp.2018.37.10.751.

2. Claire Gagne, "This Is the Average Screen Time for Kids. How Do Your Kids Measure Up?," *Today's Parent*, October 19, 2017, www.todaysparent.com/family/family-life/this-is-the-average-screen-time-for-kids-how-do-your-kids-measure-up/.

3. American Academy of Pediatrics, "Screen Time," accessed March 22, 2023, www.aap.org/en/search/screen-time/.

4. This list is taken from the recommendations on screen time on the website of the American Academy of Child and Adolescent Psychiatry, "No. 54: Screen Time and Children," last modified February 2020, www.aacap.org/AACAP/Families_and_Youth/Facts_for_Families/FFF-Guide/Children-And-Watching-TV-054.

5. Given that these resources will change over time, for the most current resources, check out to the resources tab on my website: www.juliasadusky.com/additional-resources.

6. Child Rescue Coalition, "C.R.A.M.," accessed September 23, 2022, https://drive.google.com/drive/folders/1OQRFj6z9yi7vpqeSdUox-YLLkIrh-Xjyc. This has a downloadable contract you can use with your children.

7. A study published in 2017 found that the earliest age of pornography exposure endorsed was age five. This further points to the importance of being aware of the presence of pornography in early childhood, even if that is not when it is most commonly first seen. American Psychological Association, "The Age of First Exposure to Pornography Shapes Men's Attitudes toward Women," August 3, 2017, www.apa.org/news/press/releases/2017/08/pornography-exposure.

8. National Society for the Prevention of Cruelty to Children, "Snapshot 1: Children Sending and Receiving Sexual Messages," accessed March 22, 2023, www.nspcc.org.uk/globalassets/documents/online-safety/children-sending-receiving-sexual-messages.pdf.

BIBLIOGRAPHY

American Academy of Child and Adolescent Psychiatry. "No. 54: Screen Time and Children." Last modified February 2020, www.aacap.org/AACAP/Families_and_Youth/Facts_for_Families/FFF-Guide/Children-And-Watching-TV-054.

American Academy of Pediatrics. "Screen Time." Accessed March 22, 2023, www.aap.org/en/search/screen-time/.

American Academy of Pediatrics. "Sexual Behaviors in Young Children: What's Normal, What's Not?," Healthy Children, April 1, 2019, www.healthychildren.org/English/ages-stages/preschool/Pages/Sexual-Behaviors-Young-Children.aspx.

American Psychological Association. "The Age of First Exposure to Pornography Shapes Men's Attitudes toward Women," August 3, 2017, https://www.apa.org/news/press/releases/2017/08/pornography-exposure.

Bark Blog. "What Is Age-Appropriate Sexual Curiosity?" Internet Safety Tips, December 6, 2020, www.bark.us/blog/appropriate-age-sexual-curiosity/.

Birds & Bees. "The Course," accessed March 22, 2023, https://birds-bees.com/pages/courses.

Bouris, Alida, Bethany G. Everett, Ryan D. Heath, Caitlin E. Elsaesser, and Torsten B. Neilans. "Effects of Victimization and Violence on Suicidal Ideation and Behaviors among Sexual Minority and Heterosexual Adolescents." *LGBT Health* 3, no. 2 (2016): 153–61, https://pubmed.ncbi.nlm.nih.gov/26789401/.

Campbell, Michael G. *Relatio Finalis: Synod 15—Final Relatio of the Synod of Bishops to the Holy Father, Francis, A Working English Translation from the Original Italian*, October 24, 2015, https://stmikes.utoronto.ca/wp-content/uploads/2015/12/Relatio-Finalis.pdf.

Catechism of the Catholic Church. 2nd ed. Washington, DC: United States Catholic Conference, 2000.

Child Rescue Coalition. Accessed September 23, 2022, https://childrescuecoalition.org/.

Child Rescue Coalition. "C.R.A.M." Accessed September 23, 2022, https://drive.google.com/drive/folders/1OQRFj6z9yi7vpqeSdUoxYLLkIrh-Xjyc.

Cloud, Henry. *Boundaries Updated and Expanded Edition: When to Say Yes, How to Say No to Take Control of Your Life*. Grand Rapids, MI: Zondervan, 2017.

Copen, Casey E., Anjani Changra, and Isaedmaria Febo-Vasquez. "Sexual Behavior, Sexual Attraction, and Sexual Orientation among Adults Aged 18–44 in the United States: Data from the 2011–2013 National Survey of Family Growth." *National Health Statistics Report* no. 88 (January 7, 2016), www.cdc.gov/nchs/data/nhsr/nhsr088.pdf.

Darkness to Light. "Child Sexual Abuse Statistics," n.d. Accessed March 22, 2023, www.d2l.org/wp-content/uploads/2017/01/all_statistics_20150619.pdf.

Emba, Christine. "Consent Is Not Enough. We Need a New Sexual Ethic." *Washington Post*, March 17, 2022, www.washingtonpost.com/opinions/2022/03/17/sex-ethics-rethinking-consent-culture/.

Favale, Abigail. *The Genesis of Gender*. San Francisco: Ignatius Press, 2022.

Francis. *Amoris Laetitia of the Holy Father Francis to Bishops, Priests, and Deacons, Consecrated Persons, Christian Married Couples and All the Lay Faithful*. March 19, 2016, www.vatican.va/content/dam/francesco/pdf/apost_exhortations/documents/papa-francesco_esortazione-ap_20160319_amoris-laetitia_en.pdf.

Gagne, Claire. "This Is the Average Screen Time for Kids. How Do Your Kids Measure Up?," *Today's Parent*, October 19, 2017, www.todaysparent.com/family/family-life/this-is-the-average-screen-time-for-kids-how-do-your-kids-measure-up/.

Hunt, Melissa G., Rachel Marx, Courtney Lipson, and Jordyn Young. "No More FOMO: Limiting Social Media Decreases Loneliness and

Depression." *Journal of Social and Clinical Psychology* 37, no. 10 (December 2018): 751–68, https://doi.org/10.1521/jscp.2018.37.10.751.

Ives, Kristine. "Actual Anatomy: Teaching Your Children Body Parts." Colorado Coalition Against Sexual Assault, July 21, 2015, www.ccasa.org/actual-anatomy-teaching-your-children-body-parts/.

John Paul II. *Man and Woman He Created Them: A Theology of the Body.* St. Louis: Pauline Books & Media, 2006.

Jones, Jeffrey M. "LGBT Identification in US Ticks Up to 7.1%." *Gallup,* February 17, 2022, https://news.gallup.com/poll/389792/lgbt-identification-ticks-up.aspx.

Kellogg, Nancy D. "Clinical Report—The Evaluation of Sexual Behaviors in Children." American Academy of Pediatrics, 2009, www.icmec.org/wp-content/uploads/2017/04/AAP-evaluation-of-sexual-behavior-in-children.pdf.

McLaughlin, Jessica E. "Female External Genital Organs." *Merck Manual Consumer Version.* Last modified September 2022, www.merckmanuals.com/home/women-s-health-issues/biology-of-the-female-reproductive-system/female-external-genital-organs.

McLaughlin, Jessica E. "Female Internal Genital Organs." *Merck Manual Consumer Version.* Last modified September 2022, www.merckmanuals.com/home/women-s-health-issues/biology-of-the-female-reproductive-system/female-internal-genital-organs.

Michigan State University. "Keeping Kids Safe: Warning Signs of Child Sexual Abuse." Accessed March 22, 2023, www.canr.msu.edu/creating-safe-environments/uploads/files/Warning%20Signs%20of%20Child%20Sexual%20Abuse%20Final.pdf.

Murib, Zein. "Transgender: Examining an Emerging Political Identity Using Three Political Processes." *Politics, Groups, and Identities* 3, no. 3 (2015): 381–97.

National Child Traumatic Stress Network. "Sexual Development and Behavior in Children: Information for Parents and Caregivers," April 2009, www.nctsn.org/sites/default/files/resources/sexual_development_and_behavior_in_children.pdf.

National Society for the Prevention of Cruelty to Children. "Snapshot 1: Children Sending and Receiving Sexual Messages." Accessed March 22, 2023, www.nspcc.org.uk/globalassets/documents/online-safety/children-sending-receiving-sexual-messages.pdf.

Oxford Dictionary of English. "Privacy." 3rd ed. Accessed October 2, 2022, www.oxfordlearnersdictionaries.com/definition/english/privacy.

Ryan, Caitlin, David Huebner, Rafael M. Diaz, and Jorge Sanchez. "Family Rejection as a Predictor of Negative Health Outcomes in White and Latino Lesbian, Gay, and Bisexual Young Adults." *Pediatrics* 123, no. 1 (January 2009): 346–52, pubmed.ncbi.nlm.nih.gov/19117902/.

Seladi-Schulman, Jill. "Everything to Know about Male Genitalia." *Healthline*, June 5, 2020. www.healthline.com/health/mens-health/male-genitalia.

Snyder, Howard N. "Sexual Assault of Young Children as Reported to Law Enforcement: Victim, Incident and Offender Characteristics." U.S. Department of Justice, Bureau of Justice Statistics, July 2000, nos. 1–14, https://bjs.ojp.gov/content/pub/pdf/saycrle.pdf.

Soto, Álvaro López, Jose Luis Meseguer González, Rocío López-Perez, Mónica Lorente Fernández, Juan Martínez-Uriarte, and Olivia García Izquierdo. "Sonographic Measure Techniques of Fetal Penile Length." *Obstetrics & Gynecology Science* 63, no. 5 (September 2020): 555–64, www.ncbi.nlm.nih.gov/pmc/articles/PMC7494763/.

Stringer, Jay. *Unwanted: How Sexual Brokenness Reveals Our Way to Healing*. Carol Stream, IL: NavPress, 2018.

Taylor, Susan. "Everything You Wanted to Know about Little Boys and Their Erections." Babyology, September 4, 2018, https://babyology.com.au/health/family-health/awkward-everything-to-know-about-little-boys-and-their-erections/.

Yarhouse, Mark. *Talking to Kids about Gender Identity*. Bloomington, MN: Bethany House, 2023.

Yarhouse, Mark A., Janet B. Dean, Michael Lastoria, and Stephen P. Stratton. *Listening to Sexual Minorities: A Study of Faith and Sexual Identity on Christian College Campuses.* Westmont, IL: InterVarsity Press, 2018.

Yarhouse, Mark, and Julia Sadusky. "The Complexities of Gender Identity: Toward a More Nuanced Approach to the Transgender Experience." In *Understanding Transgender Identities: Four Views*, edited by James K. Bielby and Paul R. Eddy, 101–30. Grand Rapids, MI: Baker Academic, 2019.

Yarhouse, Mark A., and Julia Sadusky. *Emerging Gender Identities: Understanding the Diverse Experiences of Today's Youth*. Grand Rapids, MI: Brazos Press, 2020.

Yarhouse, Mark A., and Julia Sadusky. *Gender Identity and Faith: Clinical Postures, Tools, and Case Studies for Client-Centered Care*. Downers Grove, IL: InterVarsity Press Academic, 2022.

Yarhouse, Mark A., and Julia Sadusky. "Gender Identity and Faith." MyCounselor Training, August 26, 2022.

INDEX

Julia Sadusky is a licensed clinical psychologist and the owner of Lux Counseling and Consulting. She also is an author, consultant, speaker, and adjunct professor. Sadusky has done extensive research in sexual development and specializes in trauma-informed care.

She earned a bachelor's degree from Ave Maria University and a master's degree and doctorate in clinical psychology from Regent University. Sadusky is an affiliate member of the American Psychological Association.

Her practice is in Littleton, Colorado.

www.juliasadusky.com
Facebook: www.facebook.com/drsadusky
YouTube: @dr.juliasadusky5716